WITH *Love,*
FROM YOUR
*Angels*

Tools and Knowledge to Help You Transcend
This Human Experience

Laura Elliott

**BALBOA.**PRESS
A DIVISION OF HAY HOUSE

Balboa Press books may be ordered through booksellers or by contacting:

Balboa Press
A Division of Hay House
1663 Liberty Drive
Bloomington, IN 47403
www.balboapress.com
844-682-1282

Print information available on the last page.

ISBN: 978-1-9822-5762-0 (sc)
ISBN: 978-1-9822-5763-7 (e)

Balboa Press rev. date:  11/06/2020

# Contents

# *Dedication*

To my two best friends in the world, who also happen to be my sisters. Linda and Kathryn, thank you for all the love and support. I can't imagine going through this Earth experience without you!

# Acknowledgement

I wish to thank Margaret McElroy, Alan McElroy, and Jean Luo for being such wonderful teachers and mentors. They were instrumental in helping me to develop my gifts so that I could bring this information through. Their continued love and support is a blessing that I'm thankful for every day.

A huge thank you to Linda Zeppa for editing my manuscript! She understood where the material was coming from and really honored my process and the voice of the Angels.

A really huge thank you to those who donated to my GoFundMe page to help me make the dream of becoming a published author a reality!

# *Preface*

The idea of a book began a long time ago. But it wasn't time yet. Something I've been trying to learn is to trust in Divine Timing. To have faith that there is Divine Timing and that it is playing a part in my life. I know it does in everyone's life, but we try to force our will on the timing of events thinking that if we don't DO something 'it' will never happen, whatever the 'it' happens to be. I've discovered that impinging my will upon timing usually leads to whatever I'm trying to do not working out. If the timing isn't in accord with Divine Timing, no matter what you do it's not likely to work out.

So here I sit, after many previous attempts to find the words that need to be written down. I feel now may be the time, that now I'm being asked by the Angels to write down their words to share on a larger scale. In my readings of late, there seems to be several messages repeated over and over as many people are having similar difficulties. The Angels ask me to pass along tools that will help us all navigate this physical experience on the Earth right now, as well as the things we need to remember to help us successfully achieve the upcoming Ascension process so that we may move on to our next Density Experience.

This book is for those that seek change, those who seek to understand why they were born and desire to reconnect with their True Selves that are still in the world of Spirit. The topics in this book are the messages the Angels have been giving through readings, channelings, and blog posts. The time has come for us to take it upon ourselves to reach out for who we truly are, the Beings of Spirit we truly are. In order to do that there are steps to follow and a process of peeling back the layers to reveal the truth that is deep inside, hidden for a while, but now ready to be revealed. Each step must be learned and mastered before incorporating the next. But every journey begins with the first step and continues as you decide to keep putting one foot in front of the other.

The Angels and I support each one of you along your journey of rediscovery of your True Self, and humbly offer the words in this book in support of that journey.

Laura

# *Preface II – A New Chapter*

This is indeed a New Chapter. So much is changing every day that you even say to yourself that you cannot believe how fast the days are going. Soon the days will speed to a blur and then they will end. Soon you will have choices before you that you never thought you would have in your lifetime. Do not turn away in fear; do not react in fear to the unknown. This is why what we wish to teach you is so important now, more than ever. There is no more putting these lessons off for another time; there will not be another time on Mother Gaia. We tell you this not to cause alarm, but to emphasize the importance of choosing to face the lessons you have chosen to accomplish. We are giving you fair warning that the time is upon you to hop off the fence, so to speak. We will be there to catch you and walk you down the path that you have chosen to follow.

The Angels

# The Illusion of Separation

When you are born, you forget. Everything. You forget who you truly are, you forget why you were born, you forget why you decided to be born on Earth. You forget that it was your choice where, when and to be born at all. You are born in total ignorance of the Universe and all whom inhabit it. You do this so that you can fully participate in a true physical 3-D experience and find your way back to the truth. As in the Wizard of Oz, it takes away the magic of the experience when you know who is behind the curtain. If you were born remembering your True Selves it would alter the physical experience. This is not how it was originally; things have gone awry and you have moved further and further from your True Selves. There was a time when you maintained the knowledge of your Spiritual Selves while you were in the physical. That time was long ago, and you have been caught in a downward spiral until you now believe that you are the physical skins you wear and question if there is anything else. Some of you are sure that when you die you will just simply blink out of existence. You have strayed so far from your True Selves that you genuinely believe you are simply the skin, bones, and mechanics of the physical body you inhabit. And to further separate yourselves, you have fallen into the belief that you are the only occupants of the entire galaxy, the entire Universe, and have even separated yourselves from yourselves. You may perceive separateness as your reality, but that does not change the metaphysical mechanics of all that the Creator has brought to life. While in the physical, it is most difficult to comprehend the vastness of spiritual energy, to understand that all is connected. It is difficult to see past the illusion that all is separate and each being is unto itself.

We offer this analogy in hopes that it helps you to understand, at least in some small way, how the connection remains even though you do not see it. We call this the 'Water Cooler' analogy. If you were to fill a pitcher of water from a water cooler (the water cooler being the Creator of All and you the pitcher) and then fill an infinite number of pitchers (the pitchers being other Beings and Entities on the Earth as well as throughout all the Universes), those pitchers would be the Higher-Selves of all things created by the Creator. Then take one pitcher (that pitcher being your True Higher-Self) and pour out a small portion into a glass. That in the glass would be the portion of you that is having a physical 3$^{rd}$ Density experience on the Earth plane at this time. If you then take your True Higher-Self pitcher and pour water into an infinite number of other glasses, that is your True Higher-Self expressing and experiencing itself in an infinite number of ways in an infinite number of places. But it is still you, because all the glasses are filled from the same pitcher, and the pitcher is filled from the water cooler. Multiply that one pitcher that is your True Higher-Self by an infinite number, too vast to express or comprehend in your current physical form, and you have an understanding of the Creator of All expressing itself in the vastness of the infinite ways it has to express and experience Itself. In this way you can see the connection of All and Everything through its connection back to the water cooler. Just because they are in different 'containers' at any given moment, they are still from the same source, and thus the same and connected. Even though you are connected to All and Everything, you will only perceive and experience separateness if you believe that to be your truth. The only way to create the change you seek is first through Awareness. You must first know you have a choice to believe something different. You cannot 'see it to believe it', you must first believe it, and only then does it come into creation. This has been shown to be true through your study of what you call Quantum Physics. You must first believe it for it to be real, not the other way around. If you wait to see it before you believe it, then you will never see it.

To expand upon this analogy, now envision a Grid of Light that runs between and through the water cooler, all the pitchers and all the glasses that have been filled, in every dimension and reality that exists. Space and time are a human perception, so we ask now that you realize this and understand that the water cooler, pitchers, and glasses are all existing at once and in overlapping realities and are connected by this Grid of Light. You are connected to All and Everything at All Times, Planes and Existences. You are never alone and have only to realize the truth of this to experience it.

This Grid of Light is an energy field that exists everywhere and all at once in all dimensions, realities, and planes of existence. It links all things and has communication as well as traveling functionality. This is not communication or traveling in the physical sense, but rather by your non-physical capabilities. This is an ability soon to be developed. There are many steps yet to achieve this capability on a large planetary scale. First, you will need to understand that it is there, that it is one of your natural abilities. This seems like a very futuristic or otherworldly ability, but we assure you, you come by it honestly yourselves. YOU are otherworldly since most of you have come to the Earth to help her and all her inhabitants free themselves from the bondage of physicality. The Earth, or Gaia, has given much to this endeavor and must now continue her path of transformation and spiritual growth. The time has come for all inhabitants of Gaia to remember their True Selves and to develop back to the Spiritual Beings that they truly are. Since you are all connected to All and Everything, what you each do or don't do affects every other living being in the Universe, including your generous and precious Gaia. Your choices not only affect yourself, but every living being in every dimension, galaxy, and plane of existence. We have all watched as you have used your promised Free Will to take your experiments to the extreme, and now, at the eve of one State of Being and the beginning of another, it is time to wake up and accept the responsibility of **'Becoming'**. This word entails so much that we choose to emphasize it. It is more than just waking to your True Self, your True Essence. It is about accepting the responsibility for all you have created that hurts others, it is about seeking to embody the concept of Service-to-Others, and it is about releasing the bondage of the concepts of the 3$^{rd}$ dimensional reality that you have embraced for so long. This existence you currently inhabit was not your original conception but a path you have strayed down due to the honoring of Free

Will. The caveat to Free Will has been reached and you will no longer be allowed to harm yourself and others. You will not be allowed to dismember yourself from the Creator (All That Is) any longer. You will no longer be allowed to harm each other and the beautiful Gaia. Many have come to save you and the beautiful Gaia from the ultimate destruction. That is not to say that you are not participants in your own saving. If you choose not to make the necessary changes, you will no longer vibrate in accordance with the vibratory level that the beautiful Gaia is transitioning to. The time to move forward is now; time is running out. Choose to ascend with the beautiful Gaia or it will be necessary for you to be transitioned to another voluntary planet, such as Gaia has been, who is going through its own growth and transition, where you will be able to continue your exploration of the truth until you are ready to take the leap back to unity with your True Self and All That Is. This is not an ultimatum, but truth and knowledge of what is to come. We wish for all to progress forward in their growth and transition back to their True Selves, but we realize not all may be ready to accept the vastness of their True Being and will need to continue their lessons. We only wish to assist in whatever way your Higher Selves deem appropriate for your Highest Good currently. This is the path we've chosen to walk - to be of assistance to our brothers and sisters having the Earth experience. It has not been an easy one and we have always been here waiting for any opportunity to jump in and offer guidance and our love. Always our love. We are blessed in this way; there have been many that have wanted to help their brothers and sisters through this experience. It is an honor that we were chosen to do so.

# *Decisions from the Heart*

You have all gotten so far away from your Heart Centers. You falsely believe that your brain should be used for decision-making and that your heart should be left out of the decision-making game completely, when exactly the opposite is true! We're not saying to totally do away with the brain in your decision-making per se, but you have gone over to that side, leaning heavily towards only brain functioning to make decisions for you. There needs to be a balance. The Universe seeks balance in all things and, naturally, so too does everything with regards to you and your well-being. We offer as an analogy the example of when you are at your most agitated, and your mind is spinning in circles from weighing options. You ask God for help, you beg and plead for the answer to be given to you, yet your mind is a frantic mess. This is like being inside a house with heavy metal music playing as loud as the stereo will allow, while we stand outside the front door knocking and ringing the doorbell. You cannot hear that we've arrived to assist you because the music is so incredibly loud. Your mind, in its frantic state, is too much a jumble with noise and fear to hear that we are answering your call for help. We, your Higher Self, and all your Guides and Helpers, speak to you through your heart.

So, just as you must turn down the music on the stereo to hear us knocking and ringing the doorbell, so too must you turn down the noise in your mind to hear us answering your call for help.

The tool we offer to achieve this is meditation. We know that your understanding of meditation may be limited; the idea that you might have is that it requires you to sit on the floor with your legs crossed and your hands held just so for a certain period of time. This is a common misunderstanding that we wish to clear up once and for all. It is not the act of meditating itself that is important, but the FEELING that is achieved during meditation. We will explain further. Meditation is any activity that allows you to relax your mind, let it wander, let thoughts come and go as they will, to find peace in the moment you are in without thinking of before or after, yesterday or tomorrow. It is about existing in the very moment you are currently in and finding peace there. For some it is a hike alone along a beautiful trail, to sit on a boulder or tree stump and just be in the moment and breathe. They do not consciously think of anything; they let their mind wander where it will. When you are only existing in the moment and finding peace and tranquility in the moment - that is when you are in meditation. That FEELING at that moment is what meditation is all about. For some this may be while sewing, or crafting, or coloring, or painting, just to name a few things that people find peaceful and relaxing, allowing them to be in the exact moment they are in and to relax their minds so that thoughts come and go as they please. Meditation is about learning to quiet your mind in this way, and it is about RELIVING that FEELING of peace at any time of your choosing. The goal of meditation is not the act of doing it, but to make it second nature so as to bring that feeling of calmness and peace to your life at any time of your choosing.

In the analogy of you being in the house with the music blaring too loud to hear us, if you were to apply the calmness and peace, experience again the FEELING of that (don't just remember it, but conjure the FEELING), your mind would quiet. You would in essence turn down the music, and you would hear us answering your prayer for guidance. We are only able to speak to you through your intuition and Heart Center. When you are in a state of panic, fear and turmoil, you immediately go out of your Heart Center and into the mind. The mind is a construct of the Lower Self. In your current reality it does have its functions and plays a necessary role, but it is YOUR CHOICE where you are going to exist; heart is Higher-Self and mind is Lower-Self. You are meant to make decisions from the heart, and the mind is there to help you function and exist on the physical plane. We tell you - you do not want your Lower Density Self making decisions for you, for it is purely a construct of the physical plane and will cease to exist when you leave this plane. The one Self that will always be truly and fully you is your Higher Self. That is the part of you that descends directly from the Creator of all, as we explained in our Water Cooler analogy.

We understand it may not feel natural for many, if not most of you, to go to your Heart Center to find the answers you seek. It is your power being taken from you that has made you become dependent on others for decisions. You have been trained to give your power over to others to make the decisions about what is best for you and how you should be doing things. But we tell you it is now time to awaken from this stupor that you have been in and to take your power back. These tools we are teaching you are meant to help you achieve just such a goal. It is your choice, and you must make it. The time is nigh for such a decision. Do not wait for others to decide first. Stand upon your own two feet and choose your own path. It may not be easy, we will not give you false tidings in those regards, but we will tell you that you are fully supported by the Universe and all the creatures in it. There are multitudes of Beings that have been waiting for the appropriate time to step up and help their Galactic family that has been separated from them for so long. There have been so many things at play that are not necessary to go into in this forum, but suffice it to say that our family has been separated for many a millennia and all are excited to welcome their Earth family back into the fold. While they are waiting to help, you must still do your part to help yourselves. You must each raise yourself and be an active participant in your rescue. As you are reaching your hands up to be lifted out of the hole of despair you have been in for too long, your Galactic family is reaching down to grab hold and pull you up. But you must first decide to do the reaching and do what is necessary to be pulled from that deep, dark hole.

# Accepting the Role of Victim

It is never too late to begin your bid for freedom. The word freedom can mean so many things, but here we mean freedom from bondage, freedom from victimhood. For too long you have allowed others to take over and control you while letting you believe that it was your idea all along. They have given you the impression that the choice you have is no choice at all, that you are a victim of circumstance, when in reality you have chosen this path and you choose to stay where you are. You are now so comfortable in your victimhood that you do not even see that it is victimhood. They have taught you to believe that this is all happening to you and that you are unable to make a choice to experience anything differently. This is a falsehood that they perpetrate and perpetuate for their gain. You have become slaves without visible bindings, but they are just as strong as the strongest bindings of the strongest alloy.

There are many ways they have found to teach you to be victims without you realizing they are doing so. One way is to teach you that there is *right, wrong, good,* and *bad* by using religion as a device to teach a moral compass. Through the weakness of man, and by taking advantage of the human failings such as the desire for power and fame, they have conveniently misinterpreted the teachings that were brought to the Earth plane to help its inhabitants remember their True Selves. Many important things have been left out of the teachings and the rest twisted to suit their needs. Their ultimate goal has been enslavement and control over the human species. By creating *right, wrong, good,* and *bad* they created **judgment**, and then decided to reinforce these teachings by saying that God judges and so it is completely acceptable and normal for humans to do the same. They even went so far as to cause fear of the Creator of All That Is by stating that the Creator of All That Is judges and judges harshly on those parameters. So they say that if you want to be accepted into Heaven then you must follow the moral compass that religion has decreed was proclaimed by God. According to those that created religion, this judging by the Almighty would culminate in 'The Last Judgment Day', convincing humans that they would stand before God and be judged for all they have done or have not done. This could not be further from the truth. The Last Judgment Day is the day humans free themselves from bondage and understand there is no need to judge themselves or any others. They understand and have full knowing that God, The Creator of All That Is, does not judge and does not require that you do either.

Let us explain this in yet another way. You may ask, "Why would we be taught to judge if it doesn't serve a purpose?" But it does serve a purpose, just not the one you think. The more fear that can be created, the more those who wish you to believe in *right, wrong, good, bad* and *judgment* like it. Fear is a device of control. All emotions stem from either fear or love, and if you are existing in fear you are not existing in love. Fear is a construct of the Lower Physical Self, whereas Love is of the Higher Spiritual True Self. When you are in fear, you are in your mind. You lose contact with your heart and intuition, and therefore your Higher Self and all your Guides and Angels for that is where we speak to you. It is desired by those that have taught you of fear to separate you from your True Self, from each other and from All That Is. They wish to bring you isolation, desolation, and loneliness. In this way you have learned to play the role of victim and come to believe that everything is happening to you and not by your choice. The first step to freeing yourself is Awareness, which you are gaining by reading this material. The second step is making the conscious choice to behave differently, to accept and forgive yourself for all the time you have spent judging yourself and others and to begin anew. This is attained through what we will call Detachment.

Most, if not all, would tell you that Detachment means you do not care about something or someone when really it means you care very much. Detachment means that you can let things, or people, be as they are, accept them as they are without the need to judge or change them. True Detachment means you don't need or require things, or people, to be a certain way. It means that you do not need a particular outcome to an event or relationship. True Detachment is freedom in the most loving way, and it is one of the best gifts you can give yourself.

While we are on this topic, let us speak of freedom and what that truly means. Freedom is joy, is love, is an opening of the heart without fear of the unknown, of what may come. Freedom is the ability to let your heart and mind wander without fear of repercussions. Freedom is what you all seek and fear that you will never find. And in considering the fear, you create what you fear. It is truly a never-ending cycle of hope and fear that never brings you closer to what you truly desire. The cycle in fact is curable, but it is your choice to be cured. Think of the tree, the plant, the blade of grass. It is what it is without considering what it is or how it came to be. They are living their truth despite all that is done to them in regard to manipulation and change. They KNOW who they are because they have not been separated as you have from the source. But still it is possible to regain that KNOWINGNESS that you have given up. Yes, you have given it up. You have given over your power to those who have convinced you that they know better. Freedom is a choice, and that choice starts with you. No one can save you but you. There are so many in the world of Spirit and the Galaxies awaiting your call. But you must ask. We may only interfere in the Free Will mandate under extreme circumstances, such as the destruction of all that live upon the planet; otherwise you must ask us each and every day to assist you in any way we can. This is an important point to remember, please. Without your invitation to intercede on your behalf we are limited as to what we can do. Even our smallest messages and nudges are often dismissed as coincidence, or as an occurrence of an active imagination. At all times we are listening for your call.

# *Belief vs Knowing*

This brings us to the topic of bridging the gap between where you are and where you want to be. When they say, "take a leap of faith", it truly means you are jumping off the edge of a chasm without knowing for sure the footing will be there. There are many ways to express this in imagery, but we like to use the image of someone standing at the edge of a cliff, a deep chasm spread between where they are and where they want to be. Some will turn and walk away because they do not see the proof of a walkway, therefore they do not believe it is there. For those that have a *knowing* of the walkway, even though they do not see it with their physical eyes, they take that first step and the walkway appears below their foot, and continues to appear as they take each step. It is their *knowing* that allows them to see. You will never believe if you need to see it first, and you will never have a *knowing* if you need to believe it first. Do you see? Therefore, it comes down to *knowing* something is real so that you can see it, rather than seeing it to know it is real.

Understanding this concept can change your life. In this understanding and *knowing* you have the ability to change your life. To create the life you wish to experience. In your *knowing* you create your reality every day. You are doing it now unconsciously. You effortlessly create a life that you find unsatisfactory because you feel that you have no choice, and you must take what life gives you. But you are in fact creating your circumstances. This may not be what you want to hear but we have promised to bring you the truth in your time of need, and the only way to create change is to have an *awareness* of what you have been choosing to do in the belief that you don't have a choice. You can just as easily create the life experience you do find satisfactory in the same way you are creating the life experience you do not find satisfactory. It involves where your focus is, on what you want or what you do not want. It all begins with *awareness* and all we have been talking about ties in together. We will attempt to sum it up for you in a list.

1. Awareness – Awareness is key to all change. Without awareness you do not realize the patterns that have been set, the cruise control you have set that takes you down the road without much thought at all. Without an awareness of the patterns and the change that is possible, there is no next step.

2. Taking your Power back – Your power has been taken away without you even being aware of it. It was given over to others who have no regard for your desires, but only have their own desire for power and control. This has put you into the victim mode we spoke of. Therefore, the next step after becoming aware that YOU DO HAVE A CHOICE, is to CLAIM YOUR POWER back in your name and to CHOOSE TO DO SOMETHING DIFFERENT than you have been doing. When you claim your rightful power and

strength, you can then realize you can choose how you feel. You realize that even though the world has an outer influence on you, you still have the power to choose how you feel; you have the power to choose love instead of fear. You all wish for peace in the world as an unattainable wish, yet we tell you that if you all reclaimed your power to choose love over fear at every turn, then you would in fact create the world of peace that you so desire. We are here to tell you that world peace is truly attainable by each person by following this advice to choose love instead of fear at every turn.

3. Breaking the old habits – You are all taught to fear; this is not a natural occurrence. As you grow and are taught to fear, you lose your sense of *knowing* and the knowledge that you have a choice not to fear. The teaching of fear is the indoctrinator of control and the loss of your true powerful Spiritual Self. Because you are taught to fear, you lose touch with your True Self and become a lump of flesh that you fear losing. If you think on it, you will realize that fear is an emotion centered around the uncomfortableness of the Physical Self, or the loss of the Physical Self that you call death (which we call Transformation). You are taught that you are the flesh you are wearing, and that when that flesh is gone then you are gone with it. In this way the fear perpetuates itself beyond all reason because you have fallen so deeply into the belief that your skin is all there is of you. You are then adding to the fear of non-existence. But this fear is the basis of all fears, is it not? When you question why you were taught this fear, and realize it was all a fabricated lie to control and

confuse you, with this awareness you can CHOOSE DIFFERENTLY. By this we mean you are not helpless to feel things, to REACT to stimuli; you are able to RESPOND by choosing not to fear. We label this step as 'Breaking the old habits' because reacting has become the norm, and changing the norm is to change a habit. At first, you will not remember, until after the fact of your reacting, that you do have a choice to respond instead. Then you will find that you begin to react and in the middle of reacting you remember that you have a choice and switch to responding instead. Next you will catch yourself as you begin to react and remember that you have the choice to respond instead. Eventually you no longer react but respond right from the beginning. And we will reassure you that the skin you now wear is only for the experience your soul is having at this moment and is not the entire Being of who you truly are in Spirit. Your current Earth experience is only as a drop of water in the vast ocean that is your True Spiritual Self experiencing itself in a vast number of ways all at the same time. This is another topic we will cover further a bit later. For now, we reassure you that the end of your existence is not something that is even possible. Even if you were to leave your current physical form, it is not the end of you; it is only the end of this current experience. You do continue on in an infinite number of other experiences that you are simultaneously experiencing in the vastness of this Universe and others.

# Finding Your Higher Purpose

So much changes before your eyes and you feel so out of control. The answers you seek can only be found within. Your Heart Center is where you are still connected with your Higher Self and where we, and all of those in Spirit, await your call for assistance. We are just a call away, but you will not notice our response to your call if you are not attuned to the Heart Space. So many of you reside in your Mind, and the Mind is the way to madness for sure. Only frustration and more questions will meet you there, and never will you find the answers you seek to life.

What is the path that you choose for yourself? For it is your own path that you have chosen - not God or any other Being, but you. In your search for your Higher Purpose, look within and connect there. For the first step in finding your Higher Purpose is remembering your connection to your Higher Self through the Heart Center. No one can tell you what your purpose is; you must do this work for yourself. It is in essence the difference between taking a trip yourself and experiencing it and someone else taking a trip and relating their experiences to you. There is much to be said for having the experience yourself, for that is truly where the rubber meets the road, as you say. Do not think twice about this; do not allow self-doubt to defeat you before you even get started. Your Ego Self or Lower Self (however you choose to refer to the physical self-realized part of yourself) will attempt to hold you back out of fear for its own existence. This is the part of you that encourages you to worry about your physical survival and needs, instead of resting in the Higher Self realization of abundance for all. This Lower Self takes self-satisfaction in accomplishing its goal of holding you back, all the time thinking it is doing the right thing. It is your *awareness* of this aspect of yourself that allows you to confront it, teach it to have Faith in your Higher Self, and to allow them to work together in harmony. Yes, your physical needs must be met while you are in this physical reality; however, with the awareness of your duality you are able to make conscious choices regarding them, rather than reacting with fear as your motivation. The two can coincide in harmony and bring you a peace and freedom that you have not known for a very long time. It is time to awaken to this duality and to the truth that you can make a conscious choice about which realm to exist in, fear or love.

We speak to you at this time and in this way to encourage you and to support you in these difficult times. We have always been here, and as much as it has pained us in our compassion for your choices and plights, we are stepping forward as the time for the experiment to end has come. The choice is upon you to live in Service-to-Self or Service-to-Others. There will be no more sitting on the fence and waiting to see what happens and tipping to one side or the other with the wind as it blows. You must now make a conscious choice and show that you are ready to move forward in your development or that you need further study and experience in the realm in which you currently reside. There is no judgment made of those of either decision, for judgment is a human frailty and a mantle that we in Spirit do not take on. Faith in yourself is something that must be learned. This is an essence that has been lost over time but can be fully recovered by each and every one of you. Why was the faith in your Higher Self lost? That is a complicated story but suffice it to say that it is not lost forever. We are outlining the steps for you to fully recover if you so choose.

# Retake Your Power, Save Yourself

Past misdeeds are now coming to light and you are entering a new time, a New World. No longer can you close your eyes and hope it will all go away once you open your eyes again. The path has been chosen and committed to, but only in so far as you are willing to carry it out. It is up to you to decide to change your path and thus the path of all upon the Earth at this time. You have the power to do this. We are here to tell you about the True Power that is yours to wield, should you choose to remember it is yours and retake it.

So many of you sit in your homes hoping that someone will come along to save you. You look to other mortals, you look to the heavens, and you look to those that you have already given your power away to, but you do not look within yourselves where you should be looking. All change begins within. You must be the change that you wish to see in the world. Just as a pebble thrown into a pond creates ripples in the water, so too is the energetic effect you have when you are the pebble that is thrown into the pond of humanity. When you change you, you change the world through an energetic ripple effect. This effect is happening whether you choose to do it consciously or unconsciously. You can vibrate out a ripple of healing that has no end to its wave, or you can ripple out fear, which is what you have been doing. The only way to change this is to change your view of yourself and to understand the True Power you wield in your environment. Everyone wields this power. But when you turn your Free Will over to those that cajole you into believing that they have the answers and you can rely on their course and their certainty of how things should be, you give over the strength that is yours to command and then live in fear because you think you are powerless. That all you can do is hope there is someone out there making decisions in your best interest. This is not the way to go about life. You are here on the Earth plane to have this experience. You chose this. Do not be frightened to look at what life has become. Do not feel guilt for the choices you made and the power you gave away. This is not the purpose of our words. We tell you this to bring awareness to you of how to create the change you wish to see and experience. The only way to do that is to point out what decision has led you to where you are now. Do not mistake our words; this is not judgment, and we encourage you not to participate in that lower vibrational energy. Simply acknowledge the new Awareness of the situation and consciously choose to make a change.

It is as a child playing with their toys. They may smash a finger, or otherwise hurt themselves, without meaning to. They experience the pain and release it, then decide to do something else, to move on and have another experience with another toy. They do not carry the pain they experienced with the one toy on to the next toy. They come to the next experience as if the other experience hadn't happened because they are able to be in each moment as it happens. Watch children and recall what it is to experience being in each moment as it happens and letting go each experience as it is completed. This is so important. At some point in your development growing up, you observe adults holding on to pain, anger, judgment, regret and other fear based emotions, and you come to believe this is the correct way to behave after having an experience. It is not. You as a child had the right of it, and you were trained the unhealthy way of existing. This is not the adults' fault; the same thing befell them as they grew from child to adolescence to adulthood. This tragic training goes too far back for you to trace and is not important to our lesson so we will not go into that here at this time. Suffice it to say, it is training, a learned behavior, that has moved you away from your True Spiritual Self having the desired experience on the Earth plane to a being full of fear who has been tricked into giving over your True Power, your True Free Will. We say tricked because you were made to believe that this was the best and only real choice, so that you believed you were the one making the choice, when really, those that tricked you were pulling the strings behind the curtains. There are always those that will find a way around a rule or law, allowing them to behave how they wish while still, not technically, breaking that rule or law. Again, we do not reveal these truths to bring anger or vengeance to your minds, but to bring Awareness. Awareness of a situation allows you to take back your True Power and to make conscious choices from a place of love, from your Heart Center. Do not hate those that have deceived you but turn to face them with love in your eyes and hearts.

Thank them for the opportunity of learning that they have provided you.

Dark and Light provide contrast for one another and are a part of the balance of the Universes. There is no judgment held for either by the Creator, for all is a valid experience in the Universes. Once you understand and experience this, you are able to check that off your list and move on to the next experience. It is all valid and wonderful, but you have become lost in the experience. We wish to awaken you and remind you that it is simply an experience you are having at this moment in this reality. It is only one of many experiences you are having simultaneously, and as each part of you is having an experience the whole of you is benefiting from it.

# Time to Awaken

What we wish to say may surprise you. It will not be what you think would come from us. But if you feel the energy of what we say, you will know that it does indeed come from us. We wish to speak to you of love and forgiveness, hatred and blame, light and dark and everything in between. There is so much that you do not remember that we wish you to. It is not an easy path that you have chosen, and certainly one that you have not chosen lightly by far. It was one that you undertook with all the graveness that was due it. Many of you reading this now will come to an understanding of who you are soon. The illusions of this 3<sup>rd</sup> Dimension will soon fade away and your eyes will behold the matrix behind the illusion. It has always been there, but a part of the game was for you to forget this. It is time for you to re-awaken and slumber no more. You have slept over-long and the time has passed for you to move forward. There can be no further delay in your trip, no more waiting for the others to catch up. You must continue your journey and they will continue theirs as they choose. It is no longer your responsibility to make sure they 'make the train in time'. Your ticket to board is waiting for you to retrieve, your seat is assigned, your journey is due to begin; it only awaits you to pack your bags and stow them on board. It is very exciting! We have all been waiting for eons for this moment to arrive and we wait with anticipation as a child waits for Christmas morning. We are the ones that have placed the presents under the tree and wait with excitement to see YOUR excitement when you open them. Will it be something you asked for or something even better? The anticipation on both sides is almost more than we all can bear, isn't it?

For some time now you have been feeling the urge that it is past time to move on. You expected it much earlier and right you were. The timing of things in the Universes is freeform however, and always occurs at the 'right' time whenever it does finally occur. There is no such thing as a wrong time, only a change of circumstances based on choices at any given moment. You do not need to concern yourselves with timing. Only know that your feelings are not wrong, have never been wrong. Do not hold onto an idea or a perceived plan because it can change at any moment. Things are reaching an apex however; where the Universe will not allow things to continue in the fashion they have been for the past millennia or so. The timing does not matter so much, as the circumstances must now change for those that have sacrificed thousands of years of their existence in service to humanity on the Earth plane as well as for Gaia herself.

So many of you do not realize that your planet, Gaia as you call her, is a living sentient Being who has made a conscious choice to support the life of humanity upon her. She has endured much abuse as of late and has delayed her ascension in service to those upon her. It is now time for her to rest, rehabilitate and recover so that she can ascend to her next level of existence. She has given much in service to those Beings upon her and many of you thank her daily, while many of you still see her as yours to do with as you will. There is no judgment in that statement, merely a neutral observation. She does wish to thank those who have sought to help her heal and who have honored her service to humanity. She wishes all well and it is her greatest desire for all of humanity to progress in the way that is for their best and highest good.

So many of you also do not realize that your plants, rocks, trees, and animals are all sentient Beings with their own souls and levels of consciousness. They have chosen to be co-creators with Gaia in her ascension process as part of their own ascension process. They have also chosen to be a part of humanity's growth process. Even though they are treated as 'things' by humanity, they also contain the essence of the One Infinite Creator and as such are an expression of the One Infinite Creator experiencing Itself. Unlike humanity, they DO remember their connection to All That Is and even though they are treated as 'less than' and used shamelessly by the human population as a whole, they only hold love and compassion for humanity. As a part of the One Infinite Creator, they are a part of the Universal Consciousness and communicate with each other and the Universe as a whole. It is humanity that has forgotten their connection and is now striving to remember it. All these Beings are speaking to you in your heart, but you are too much in your mind and walking around with amnesia to hear them. Just because you do not hear does not mean they do not speak. It is up to you to remember your connection with the One Infinite Creator and to begin listening with your heart to the Universe around you. There is so much life happening around you that you are not aware of because you have chosen to keep your blinders on out of fear of the unknown, out of fear of what you might see, hear, or feel if you were to take them off. You pretend that nothing exists outside of your current field of vision, and so far, have completely succeeded in convincing yourself that this is true. As a cart driver may put blinders on the pair of horses pulling the cart so that they are not frightened or distracted by what is going on around them, so too have you left your blinders on. But unlike the horses, you can take your blinders off and look around yourself. You must be willing to face the fears that are unknown to you. Whether it turns out to be a couple of harmless bunnies that were outside your field of vision or a bear ready to charge, you must come to the understanding that you are capable of handling any situation. Stand in your power and have confidence in the knowledge of your True Self that is revealed upon removing the blinders. That knowledge of your True Self is the reward for facing your fears and removing the blinders. It is not possible to put the cart before the horse - you cannot know for sure what is or is not there before you take the blinders off. You must trust in your Higher Self, your Higher Power, and remove the blinders without the prior knowledge of what lies beyond. In so doing, in facing your fears to expel them, you find the true meaning of courage and strength. In that moment your life is changed forever. You will never be the same again. Once you accomplish this feat you will never be the same, you will never be able to go back. But that is a good thing. Once you overcome fear and see it from the other side you will not want to go back, for you will then understand all. The reward for facing your fears is understanding, and once you have that understanding you know the necessity of fear but also of learning to overcome it. It is then that your life changes and you become the ripple in the quiet pond that extends out to every corner of not just the world but also the Universes. Every change you make in yourself creates that ripple in the Universes. There is no place that the ripple ends; there is no shore for it to crash upon to end its journey. Each and every one of you is that significant. You have forgotten so much, and we are here to remind you of what you once knew and of the powerful Spiritual Beings that you truly are. This power has never gone away, it simply awaits you to reclaim it and wield it with Unconditional Love, Forgiveness, and Non-Judgment of yourself and all. For when you are these things to yourself you are also them to others; when you are to others, you also are to yourself. You are all one and the same energy, vibration, part of the One Infinite Creator having this experience. We ask that you no longer be lulled into the complacency and stupor of the 3rd Dimension that you have chosen to inhabit for a time. We are here, as requested, at the requested time, to awaken you from your slumber, from the nightmare you have been experiencing, to help you awake refreshed, renewed, and ready to get dressed and start your beautiful day. Allow us to prepare your way. We will start the coffee, put some bread in for toasting, squeeze some oranges for orange juice, make all your favorite breakfast items, and by the time you are up and out of the shower your meal will be prepared and ready for you to sit among us and break bread. We have longed so for this moment and are so excited that it has finally arrived! The kitchen is bustling with activity and we await you at the table so that we may begin our meal together.

# Time to Progress Beyond this Experience

Half of the planet is free from terror, and the other half is ensconced in it. What if those two were to merge somewhere in the middle and the fear was overcome by the joy and lightness of Being? Well that is what is happening now. You do not see what occurs when you are in the middle of it, but take hope in the knowledge that we look over you and endeavor to help you awaken to the True Beingness of yourselves. The path is wrought with potholes and unseen dips and grooves, and even though your footing is unstable, we hold you upright along your way. The day will come when you remember all and the support we have lent you will be taken over by you and you will then turn to those coming up the path behind you and you will be the ones offering the support and guidance along the path. It is the way it has always been. Have faith in that knowledge and that you do not face this climb alone.

Many years have passed since you were truly at One with the Creator in your minds, but that is a part of the illusion of separation that you are currently experiencing. Never have you been separate; it is in no way possible for that to actually happen. It is only where you are standing that allows you to have this perception. Change your standpoint and change your perception. All it takes is one shift in either direction and the view of your surroundings will change forever. For once you see you cannot un-see. Once you know, you cannot un-know. The knowledge is there even if you have currently forgotten it is there.

Do not fret the remembering but embrace each experience that brings you closer to that remembering. Every experience you have is valuable in that it moves you back to your True Being by design. It is all a part of the process that you desired to experience and what brought you to this planet from many different places. Most of you are not originally from here, from Earth. You have come to help your brethren along that path, as you once were helped along. As others have sacrificed years of their existence to aid you, you now have given years of your existence to help those coming along. It is how it is meant to work in the Universes. The Development of One affects the Development of All because One and All are the same. Do you see? We attempt to explain a process of non-separateness to those that only perceive separateness, to those that believe that anything outside of their physical flesh is not them, to those who see the flesh they currently wear as their actual Being, as the limit of their self-expression, to those who see their flesh as a barrier against the rest of the world, the rest of existence. It is time to move beyond this false belief. In order to progress to your next set of desired experiences, you must release the idea that you are the flesh you currently wear. You must now realize that the flesh you currently wear is but a suit that you have dressed in to go out on this trip you have taken to the

Earth. It is as if you were packing for a trip, for a vacation, and you must decide what to wear while you are away. This skin you currently wear is but an outfit you have chosen to wear for your trip to this Earth plane. It was chosen with care so that you might have the experiences you desired while on your trip. Eventually, when your trip is complete, you come home and change back into your comfortable clothes. When you come home to Spirit, you are welcomed; you change and make yourself more comfortable, and put away your traveling clothes for another time. Nothing changes as far as your True Essence; you simply change clothes. Such is it when you come home to Spirit; you change out of what you donned for your trip (the physical flesh) and change back into the form you are most comfortable in.

So many are confused about their return Home. They have become so wrapped up in their trip that they have forgotten they are even on a trip and have come to think of the trip as Home. We have house-sat and watered your plants while you have been away, but eventually you must return and care for them yourself. That is why we remind and assure you that you are indeed only on a trip and that your Home awaits you when you have completed your experience.

The thought that you have simply taken a trip, and forgotten you have a Home, may seem odd to you. You are saying to yourself that you would not take a vacation to Hawaii and forget you live elsewhere, so why would you do that in any other circumstance? But we tell you, you have. You have completely forgotten your real Home so that you could completely immerse yourselves in the experience of the trip. If you remembered you were only visiting and had a Home to return to, it would affect the results you desired to achieve. But now we remind you and help to bring your memories back, as you requested us to, because it is time to remember that you have a true Home, and this is not it. Do not be frightened by this message. When you open the doors to your Home and walk inside you will feel the joy of setting down your things, kicking off your shoes, and plopping down on the couch as if after a long day away. It will be comforting and soothing to be Home again, and you'll wonder at whatever it was that enticed you to leave in the first place.

We wish to assure you that returning Home is as wonderful as that sounds. You fear death because you do not remember that you are more than the suit of flesh you are currently wearing. You are afraid that there is nothing after this, and when you lose your suit of skin you cease to exist. This is the ultimate form of disassociation and denial of your True Self. To have gone so far, fallen so deeply asleep to your True Self, is another thing all together. Those that have moved so far away from their centers in one sense are also closer to the truth than they realize. The further you are from yourself the closer you are. If you are circling, if everything is in constant motion, if everything that goes out comes back to you, in this respect the further you are from the beginning the closer you are to it as well. This path is necessary for some, not all, but some choose this experience and share it with the Collective Consciousness as a valid experience in the Universes.

There are many paths that lead to the same ending point, and all are valid paths to reach the same location. Do not judge the paths of others as not as good or valid as your own, because then you fall prey to the lower vibrational energy that judgment brings. All are sharing their experiences with the Collective Consciousness, of which you are also partaking. So, when you are judging others, you are also judging yourself, and that energy of judgment affects all as the low vibratory rate it inhabits is spread throughout the Collective Consciousness. There are those that work so hard to increase and maintain the vibratory rate of the populace. As climbers, seeking to climb the mountain, place safety hooks to help hold the position as they go, so too are there those among you who serve as the safety hooks to hold the gain that is achieved in your climb towards Awakening. Everyone plays their part; there are no small bits in this play; every actor is valuable and has an important role to play for the benefit of all. Every life is important, every choice important, every move from fear to love is important. There is no shoreline to stop each ripple that is created, so we wish you to create your ripples in the water with the clear intent of love and the best and highest good of all. Only then will the world around you change.

The world around you is a reflection of your inner world. As within, so without. You will never be successful in making changes in your world until and unless you first begin making the changes needed within yourselves. If you keep trying to make the changes outside yourself without first making the changes within, you will never succeed in making the changes that you wish to see in the world. You will continue to see more of the same. If you keep doing what you have been doing, you will keep getting what you have been getting. Recognize that what you have been doing is not working, and take these suggestions we offer to help you create the change in the world that you wish to see. When you make the internal change, vibrationally it ripples out with no end, meeting up with other ripples and crashing together and blending. None is destroyed but instead all continue in a never-ending wave. The higher vibrational wave will include the lower vibrational wave and lift it to new heights. In order for your vibrational wave to stay in a higher vibration, the wave must be sent out containing Unconditional Love, Forgiveness, and Non-Judgment. Only in that way are you able to hold the higher vibration that is able to transmute the lower vibrational rates of those that are not holding that space. If you are able to hold that higher vibrational space, than you are able to assist others in raising their vibratory rate to meet yours, rather than meeting them on a lower vibration and attempting to drag them back up with you. Hold your higher vibrational rate and those around you will begin to raise theirs to meet yours.

# We are Your Safety Net

As in the past, the future holds many opportunities and possibilities. The choice you make now will have an everlasting effect on the landscape of your existence. Why do you fret about daily activities when such a momentous decision awaits you? Because you are not aware of the momentous decision that is before you. You are completely wrapped up in the Earthly dramas that inhabit your daily existence and have forgotten your true reason for being here now as you are. We are here to help you with this, as requested. Many lifetimes ago you came to us and told us of your dreams, the possibilities you wished to experience for the collective. It was your joy to participate in this undertaking. Somewhere along the way the joy was lost. The further you strayed into the experience, the further away you drew from your Source and the true Reality of the Universes. We are your failsafe. You asked us to keep an eye on your progress and to monitor the situation and if necessary, at the most correct time for your experience, to bring you back to your fullness in memory and in form. We have promised to do this and so we have arrived at this time to help you return to your Source, to your True Selves.

This is no easy task. We remind you outright of your

request and yet not only do you refuse to listen to our messages and reminders, you have ceased to believe in the messengers. Some of you have strayed so far from your Core Essence that you ceased to even acknowledge the Creator's existence and came to believe you are a product of evolution. While in some respects this may be true, it is not true in the way that you believe. You seeded this planet and, combined with the life force that was here, developed from that seed. So, in essence, you are partially correct, but what you believe is not the full explanation of your existence. This is one of the things you wished for us to remind you of, should you fall so deeply into your slumber that you forget. We are here to say, you have forgotten. It is your choice, as always, how far to carry your experience of separation, but there really is no further to go as you have denied your True Self your origin, and your Creator. There is no way to separate yourself further than you already have. So, we say it is time to remember and to move on to your next chosen experience. There is nothing further to be gained in this arena. All have reached their fill of this experience and require no further denial of their True Selves. As we have previously said, you are not the only one having this experience. You hold the space for many souls in the Collective Soul Groups who are also learning from your experience of separation. It is now becoming painful for all to observe and the experiment can no longer be allowed to continue.

We have dreamt of the day that you would return home to us in the full Beingness and Highest Expression of your True Selves. This is the way and the time. We have come as promised to help you in this, but it is also your choice and takes work on your side to return things to as they were before. Not in the sense of before having the experiences you have had, but a return to your True Beingness while incorporating the Experiences of your journey upon the Earth in 3rd Density. Those Starseeds that have come to be by your sides have been encapsulated in this Dimension and Density with you for many eons, as they have been unable to leave their duties here while you have been kept safe during your requested experiences and attempt to return yourselves to the Collective.

This did not happen as planned, and now must be adapted to current situations that have arisen. The Starseeds that are here are weary and long to return to their homes to rest and recuperate for it has been a long haul. They have loved humanity so much, their brothers and sisters whom they saw suffering in the experiment of separation. They chose to stay and offer comfort, even though many times over the centuries they were persecuted and condemned for their strange ideas and abilities. They still returned on each cycle to bring love and light to humanity so that it would never be forgotten from whence they came, their True Creator Source Being. This is not related to bring about any such feelings of guilt or sadness, but instead to bring Awareness to humanity of those who have served among you for the many eons of your existence. We tell you this because it is now time to awaken to their presence fully and to seek them out for their guidance back to the One Infinite Creator. Many of you, more than ever before, have felt this draw to those who in the past have been deemed witches, or otherworldly in knowledge and demeanor. These are the ones that have retained the knowledge for humanity, to replant it when the time was right to awaken. This is that time. Many of those Starseeds are awakening to their True Nature, while always knowing that they were different and had abilities that were more developed in them than in other members of society. They are now remembering their True Selves and where they originally came from to help humanity on the Earth.

It has been very difficult for Starseeds serving here on the Earth. They have longed for home and souls that they have not been able to exist with for many eons. It is as for you when you go on a long work trip and haven't had any contact with your friends and family for a very long time. So it is for the Starseeds upon Earth who have been missing their Soul Families. They may not have always known what that empty feeling was that they were experiencing, but at times it causes a great loneliness for them. Even so, they have been committed to their mission to help humanity during this long period.

Many thought 2012 would be the cataclysmic time of change, and so it was meant to be; but circumstances forced things to change and we wished humanity to have a little longer to choose their Polarity as this would affect their next destination and experience. With the agreement of the Earth and the serving Starseeds, this plan was implemented and has now almost reached completion. There will be no further extension of the deadline, and each soul in humanity must weigh in on one side of Polarity or the other. Will you choose Polarity of Service-to-Self or Service-to-Others? This is no small decision, as it will affect so much moving forward. Each choice is left up to each individual soul to decide. There is no judgment for those choosing either Polarity; it is simply a fact that one must be chosen in order to know which direction on the game board you wish to move, to know which play you would like your starring role to be in next.

Eventually, all is returned to the Creator because there is nothing else. There is no 'wrong' choice, only that a choice must be made. If you would like to continue your experiences in a 3rd Density reality, you will do so by remaining undecided or leaving necessary experiences unfinished. You will then continue to have the experiences related to 3rd Density reality. If Polarity of Service-to-Self is chosen, those souls will move on to a long and painful experience reaping of what they have sown. If, however, you choose to move on to your next experience, you will be choosing the Polarity of Service-to-Others. That is the Polarity that contains the necessary vibrational energy to move on to the next Density experience. Again, there is no judgment as far as one or the other. Any decision simply leads to another experience that you will be having, just as any decision you make on the Earth plane at this time only leads to an experience you have. Neither is *good* or *bad*. Inherently, all decisions lead to neutral outcomes; it is only your judgment of *good* or *bad* that makes them so. So too is your decision on Polarity. Each side of Polarity simply leads to a string of experiences that are neither *good* nor *bad,* and should be viewed as the neutral experiences that they truly are. We only wish to give you the Awareness of your Choices so that you may make an informed decision. All are different roads that eventually lead back to the Creator. It is more a matter of how long or painful you wish to make your journey.

# The Light Spectrum that is Love

Love, dear ones, is the answer to all. It spreads like wildfire in dry tinder once it is lit. It spreads jumping and leaping over hill and dale and chasms wide and deep. This is not questioned when seen in action. Love will burn down all signs of hate and ill will that have built up like a wall around you. It will burn said hate and ill will until all is put asunder. There is nothing that can withstand the force that is Love.

This simple fact is what is important to remember when coming face to face with hate and ill will. Trust in the strength of Love, know it can withstand even the harshest winters, the strongest storms, and overcome the highest mountains. We speak of this during these times of upheaval to remind you of the best way to overcome your darkest days. For some reason, the last solution you think of is Love, if it is thought of at all. You attempt to conquer hate and anger with hate and anger of your own. This will never work and is pure folly. In our wildfire analogy, it is in essence the same as adding more fuel to the fire, adding more oxygen giving the flames fuel to feed on creating a conflagration. Responding to hate and anger with Love is the only way to suck the oxygen away from the fuel starved flames and they soon extinguish because they are no longer being fed fuel but being denied what they need to continue their existence. Do you see? In the same way if someone is standing before you spewing hate and anger in your face, if you respond in kind it adds fuel to the fire and before you know it you have a full conflagration on your hands. If, however, you stand before the hate and anger and only respond with Love, the hate and anger is starved of the fuel it requires to continue or grow larger becoming out of control and instead dies out from lack of oxygen.

This is the lesson we wish you to take from these words. You have already tried responding in kind and have reaped the results of this folly. It is now time to try something different to achieve different results. If you keep doing the same things you will keep getting the same results. Responding in this way will feel very unnatural and be very difficult at first. Your first knee jerk reaction is to yell back at someone who is yelling at you. But we tell you this is NOT your natural state of Being, but something that has been trained into you. Someone who is kept in anger and hate is someone who has given their power away and strikes out in their misery. So, you are all, in essence, striking out at each other in hate and anger because of your shared misery but you do not even realize that in this expression of your pain you are only hurting yourselves. You do not even realize that what you are interpreting as a difference between you is actually a common denominator in your existence on the Earth plane. If you would but only stop for a moment and see this, then it would be much easier to find compassion for yourself and others in your shared plight and choose to respond with Love rather than reacting out of habit and misinformation.

This is so important. It may seem like a small point we make but it is a very important step in your development and the first step of many towards your growth and expansion of Being. The longest trip always begins with the smallest of steps, but once upon the path it is only by choice that you detour from that path. The true courage comes in the decision to take that first step along the path of growth and enlightenment. It is not all flowers, butterflies, and beautiful string music along the journey. We wish that it were, but we would be doing you a great disservice to not disabuse you of that concept of Enlightenment. Those that begin the journey down that path will feel discouraged when they come across their first obstacle to get around. And there will be obstacles, but we tell you none are insurmountable. It is so important to remember that all of us in Spirit are here to help you, but you must also remember to ask for our intervention due to the Free Will given to you by the Universe. We are ever by your side and responding to your requests. We are there during your darkest hours helping to hold you up to face another day.

This is one of the times that meditation plays such an important role. You must be able to drop into your Heart Center to communicate clearly with us. We are always speaking to you, but if you are unable to tap into your Heart Center you are hampering our efficacy in communicating with you. There are many ways we attempt to communicate but by far your ability to meet us at least halfway in your Heart Center is the most efficient and accurate.

Being able to drop into your Heart Center is also the only true way to exist at all times in the realm of Love. This is where you find the strength and effectiveness to respond to hate and anger with Love. This blinding all-encompassing Love shines out of your Heart Center in a blinding ray of lovely white, pink and green rays of light. The more practiced you are at executing this maneuver the more rays of light are incorporated until you are exuding pure rainbow light, which enables the receiver to accept the ray most needed to use for their best and highest good.

Never doubt your ability to do this, you are at your core and essence a Being of Light incorporating all colors of the spectrum at all times. This is a part of your remembering, of taking your power back and becoming a whole Being again. This is a piece of remembering your True Selves to experience your Wholeness once again.

# Be in Service to Others

The path to the Light is never an easy one. There are trials and tribulations you must overcome in the 3$^{rd}$ Density realm. Many of you came to Earth knowing you would be digressing for a time in an effort to lift your brothers and sisters in Spirit to the Higher Realms. You have come to bring Light to a Dark situation and serve in the most dense and difficult situations and circumstances. Just because one is associated with Dark Ones does not necessarily mean they are there to participate in the Darkness themselves, but rather to be in a position to lift those that are ready from the Darkness to the Light, to help show them the way. This is a difficult service to perform and another paramount reason not to judge others for their decisions and paths. Many serve in ways you cannot conceive, and are judged harshly for their service by those without understanding. This does not affect them or their mission, but the act of judgment does affect those who are doing the judging.

What path have you chosen that you have made no mistakes, as you perceive them? Yet you judge others for their perceived mistakes. All is a part of the plan that you have each set for yourself before coming to the 3$^{rd}$ Density Earth plane. There is no such thing as a mistake; everything is planned and timed according to Divine Timing. In your limited view as a Soul encased in the form of flesh, you do not recall this and so we are here to lovingly remind you. Do not fret upon the stage of life the decisions you have made, but thank your Higher Self for the opportunities you are receiving for growth and expansion.

You ARE still connected to your Higher Self, your True State of Being, your Divine Essence. Even if you do not recall this connection, it does exist and there is no way to disconnect from it, only forgetfulness for a time. It is your human perception of how things 'should be' that lead you to this false concept of 'mistakes'. Again, we come back around to judgment. 'Mistakes' are from the lower vibrational energy of fear. Experiences are deemed mistakes when the outcome is not the one you desired. Therefore, that outcome is deemed *bad* or a 'mistake' and then you experience all the feelings associated with the designation of *bad* and 'mistake'. Do you see? It is only judgment of the outcome of the experience that makes it so. If you are able to release that judgment, then you are able to see it was simply a neutral thing that came from the decision that was made. And then you move on to the next experience, and the next, and the next, and the next... and you get the idea.

This applies to everyone, so the ones that you think are making poor decisions and life choices are simply living out the plan they have set for themselves. Sometimes souls choose to experience the polar opposite of what they experienced in other lifetimes. Sometimes a soul will play a role as a sheriff in one lifetime and in the next lifetime will explore the other side of that coin and be a criminal. Both are just as valid. No matter how dark the soul, the only one you injure with the placement of judgment is yourself. You may notice at times that when you express anger towards someone and they do not accept or take on that anger, you are left feeling angry still or perhaps even more so. Because the other person is not responding the way you think they should by being angry back, you become even more angry. They walk away and go about their day, while you still walk around with a knot in the pit of your stomach and a sense of incompletion because the person did not yell back and give you the opportunity to completely express your anger. So, then the anger is either bottled up inside or released upon another unsuspecting person who comes into your vicinity. It is not about what the other person does or does not do in response to your anger; their response or reaction reflects on their personal and spiritual growth. What you do or how you feel is a reflection on your own personal and spiritual growth. You are all just interacting together, each in your own personal play that intersects at times with the personal plays of others. How someone responds or reacts to you is never about you, and how you respond or react to someone else is never about them. Your *stuff* is your stuff and their *stuff* is their stuff. You are only interacting to learn your own lessons and to awaken your own self from the deep sleep you have all fallen into when coming into this 3rd Density reality.

It is truly up to each and every one of you to change the world by first changing yourself. As you perfect your role in your own play, you energetically assist others to master the roles in their own plays. There is no way to stop the ripple in the pond once it starts. You can only send out more after it and you choose, each and every time, what energy that ripple will contain. Will you serve as the beacon of light amidst the darkest among you or will you stay asleep existing in the Fear and Hatred that is the lesson of the 3$^{rd}$ Dimension? While you have accepted the mantle of victimhood thus far, it is always your choice to stay that path or to Awaken to the knowledge of your True Self and release it.

We have come this far with you because we have faith in you and your ability to find yourselves. As well do all those who have come from other Stars in the Universes to assist you in your time of great and extreme growth in Awareness. All the Universes await to see your success because all is connected, and what you do, or do not do, affects all in existence. You are not alone in this journey; your experiences and learning and growth are shared with ALL. As one reaches the top of the ladder with the assistance of those above them, so too does that one then turn to help the ones coming up the ladder behind them. The ladder is an analogy, there is no above or below in development. The numbers assigned to dimensions and densities are assigned to make them easier to understand, particularly to those that exist within a linear time frame concept. In actuality there is no *above* or *below*, there is no one that is better than another, because of the density or dimension they have reached. You only perceive it that way due to your current limited perspective in this human form. Perhaps a better analogy would be a school setting, where those in lower grades are assisted on to the next grade by those who have already passed that grade and moved onto the next grade of learning but return to help those coming up behind them to learn the material that they have learned and mastered.

In helping others who are going through what you have already experienced, you are also practicing

Service-to-Others, which is a necessary polarity to continue your growth and expansion back to the One Infinite Creator. This concept of turning to help another is practiced not only by those that have moved onto other Densities (grades/ classrooms) and return to help those coming up behind them, but also by those that are still sharing the same Density (grade/classroom) but have progressed in their lessons and help their classmates study and learn the material. Helping others to remember their True Nature, their True Selves, is always a part of being of Service-to-Others. Even Jesus, who is now a part of Unity Consciousness, is still reaching out to help. While he is no longer able to lower his vibration sufficiently to inhabit a human form, he is nevertheless still accessible to all through that Unity Consciousness and speaks to you through your Heart Centers.

While Jesus is not physically among you to help with this Awakening, there are many among you who have graduated from the class you are currently in but chose to come to the Earth School to be 'tutors', or 'teaching assistants' and assist others in learning the material necessary to Awaken and 'graduate'. While these 'tutors' or 'teaching assistants' attended schools in other Universes, the 'curriculum' is the same in all of them. They have offered to be of service at the Earth School to help those here to learn the materials and be able to graduate as they did. Those of you who are the tutors, know that your time of rest arrives soon. It has been a long stretch for you without a chance to go home and rest between classes, but the opportunity will soon be offered for you to do so.

# Remove the Blinders from Your Spiritual Sight

With this time that we have with you, we endeavor to pass along as much knowledge as possible in the time allowed us. We are ever at your sides, but you do not always comprehend our presence with you. We have become an abstract thought to you, something surreal and only experienced in the chapels of Europe with a particular form and visage that you have become comfortable with. While we do not mind this assumption of our appearance, we will say it has been misinterpreted by viewers of times past who found this the only way that they could comprehend, interpret, and represent our Light Body images.

We only mention this because we wish you to open your mind and heart to the possibilities of experiencing us in any form, including our true form. You have limited your focus of us as would a horse with blinders on that only experiences what is directly before it. Blinders were put on the horses to help keep their focus trained forward and not be startled by what might be happening on either side of them. But there is so much more occurring to either side of them that they are missing. While this certainly may have its purpose at times, we say to you this is not the way to go through the experience of life.

As with the horses, if you were to remove the blinders that have been placed on you, you would then be able to perceive the great many things happening around you that you had previously been unaware of. You would also see that the sounds you were hearing and not understanding were really not to be feared but only scary because you could not see what they were or where they came from. In this line of thought we would like you to understand what our True Essence is, because it is also one that you share. By having a better understanding of our True Nature, you also have a better understanding of yours.

Deep in your past the Angelic Beings came into creation, created by the Creator as companions to the One True Infinite Being in an outer expression of Itself. We became the protectors of the Universes and the inhabitants within. We learned the secret of creation and began to co-create with the One Infinite Being who was the Father/Mother/Life-Giver that brought us into Being. We learned to create the beautiful things that would help us to experience ourselves in different forms having different experiences. In this way the One Infinite Creator was also given the gift of experience through our Creations, because all is forever and in all-ways connected to the One Infinite Creator Being.

We were all blessed by this experience and sang in joy for our Existence among all that we created. At some point, some chose to experience the duality of joy, just to see what that would be like. It was a difficult separation for all of us, but we supported each other's visions for experientiality to the fullest and wished each many blessings in their pursuit of their chosen Experience. While not all chose to Experience duality in the same fashion, that did not mean we would not all Experience it. As those of you who currently exist in the 3rd Dimension have forgotten, we are not separate Beings. You perceive your skin to separate you from everything outside of that skin, but we are all always connected, there is no way for us not to be. We all come from the same Source and are forever connected to that Source no matter what 'suit' we put on to go out and have an Experience. In this way, we all learn from the Experiences the others are having as first hand Experiencers of Duality, those who volunteered to 'go into the trenches' to give us that Experience. It is not an easy task to play the role of the hated and reviled one, and those that volunteer for those roles are very brave indeed and deserve our most loving compassion and gratitude for the role they are playing for us.

We have great compassion for those that volunteer to play the most difficult roles. They are usually perceived as 'fallen', or from below, and have been on the receiving end of much condemnation over the past eons by those that have not understood the sacrifice these Ones have made for all of us. It has been said that those in your Earthly life who are your worst enemies are your best friends in the world of Spirit. This is certainly true. Those that love you the most in Spirit are the ones that have volunteered to come and play a difficult, but necessary, role in your life. Sometimes this is on a personal basis, and sometimes on a worldly basis. These Soul Beings have volunteered for this work, knowing that they will have a difficult Experience on the Earth plane, full of condemnation and hatred towards them.

This concept also extends out on a larger scale to

the perceived 'fallen' Angels. There is no Judgment or Condemnation from God for any Experience that is chosen. Man, (and we do say Man because it has been the male of the human species that has primarily aspired for the false power over others that is perceived on the Earth plane), has taken the knowledge given them of the Divine, and placed their limited human perspectives on what occurred in the 'Heavens', as it has been referred to. They have taken some of the Creations of the One Infinite Creator and labeled them 'Fallen' and thereby separate from the One Infinite Being. As we have stated there is no separation from the One Infinite Creator; it is a complete impossibility. As well there is no *above* and *below*. These are human perceptions of things that are difficult to grasp in the limited 3rd Dimensional reality. We wish for you to understand that this concept is the same, be it 'Fallen' Angels or someone you perceive to be your worst enemy here in your physical life. These Beings are simply experiencing a duality for the benefit of all of Creation. This is actually a much harder role to play than being the *good guy*, because they are usually so reviled and hated. Which is why they are so deserving of your compassion, understanding, non-judgment, and unconditional love. These Beings have volunteered to be hated, to play the hardest role of all in this Universe, all because they Love you so deeply and completely. We who are on the *Light* side of the coin really have the easy part in the play. We are loved and kind words are always spoken of us. It is our brethren, however, who deserve the praise and compassion that has been given to us, for they have the difficult roles in the play and we have the easy roles.

This is a part of your lesson of Unconditional Love,

Forgiveness, and Non-Judgement of yourselves and others. This is SO important! We cannot stress this enough. Choosing that some are not worthy of love, but deserving of scorn because of the choices they make or have made, is NOT unconditional love. You must examine everywhere in your life where you have deemed some worthy of love and some worthy of hate, dislike, or not loving. Even neutrality towards another is not acceptable as it is not Unconditional Love. An absence of feeling leaves a void that will be filled with nonsense, whether you realize it or not. Even if you do not agree with someone or think what they are doing, or not doing, is vile, the challenge we offer you is to still exist in your Heart Center and to Love them Unconditionally. As Jesus would, as Buddha would, as any of the Teachers that have come to help humanity would. If you are judging others, even the littlest bit, then you are not Loving them Unconditionally. And if in your mind you are thinking of a teacher that has started a religion on the Earth that says differently, then they were not a Teacher of the Law Of One; they were not teaching what the Creator would have you remember but were serving their own human agendas.

Understand we bring you this information at this time because it is now that you must remember it. So many lessons have been turned to the humans' advantage in order to gain control of the masses and to keep those who desire Earthly power in control. It is now that you must awaken to your True Nature, to understand that you are Divine Beings currently having this Experience, and an Experience is all it is. When you go to Disneyland you know you are on a trip to have a good time, to experience the rides and adventures and then to return home. You plan your trip ahead of time:

how you will get there, where you will stay, what friends you will go with, what rides you will go on, what clothes you will wear etc. The Earth Experience, your trip to the Earth plane, is exactly the same thing! You planned your trip ahead of time: how you would get there, where you would stay, what friends you would go with, what rides you would go on, what skin (clothes) you would wear. But unlike your trip to Disneyland, you have forgotten that you are on a trip to Earth and that it is not your home.

Imagine if you went to Disneyland and began to think it was your home! Imagine thinking that all the crazy experiences you had while you were at Disneyland was just the way the world was and you had no control over it, and that if you left Disneyland then you would cease to exist. This sounds silly, does it not? Yet this is exactly what you have done while taking your trip to the Earth. We tell you, it is just as silly thinking Earth is all there is and that it is your whole world and you would just cease to exist if you left there. We do not mean to sound harsh but wish you to understand, with loving compassion, the extent to which you have forgotten your True Selves. It is as if you've walked into Disneyland, after journeying there by plane, car, or bus (i.e. being born to Earth through your mother's birth canal), and once inside you forget how you came to be there. Suddenly this is all that you remember as being *real*. You wear the clothes you decided to take for your trip (e.g. what skin color or gender you chose to wear this lifetime), you see to all your physical needs such as shelter, food, transportation (i.e. where you live to best support the goals for your journey), and you are with friends to enjoy the trip and help you have the experience that you desire (i.e. the friends and enemies that help you accomplish the goals and lessons you have chosen for this lifetime).

If you understand this analogy, then you see how silly it would be to go to Disneyland and then think that that is where your home is. We do not say this to make you feel ashamed or any such emotion. We say this only to help you see and realize, to become AWARE that your trip to Earth is no different than a trip to Disneyland. You are only there for a short time; you are on this trip for the experiences that you can have; you are on this trip to experience Duality first hand; you are on this trip for the benefit of yourself, but also those that you have travelled there with. And then you will return home with all the souvenirs from your trip: pictures, t-shirts, mugs, key chains, and many memories to share.

In this way, we wish you to understand that what you are experiencing on the Earth plane is but a fleeting moment in your True Existence. You have gotten so carried away with taking this Earth Experience as the one and only experience you will ever have, that you have lost the perspective of your True Higher Self. You have put blinders on yourself and restricted your view of your True Existence. It is up to you to remove those blinders and to look around you and become Aware that you are simply on a trip and nothing around you is real or lasting. Just as you leave Disneyland and go home and everything that happened there no longer affects you, so too will you go Home after this trip to Earth and soon what happened on that trip will no longer affect you. What we are asking of you is to realize NOW that you are on a trip to Earth and to understand that what is happening around you is not really real. Just as Disneyland puts on shows and has characters walking around for your entertainment, so too do you have daily occurrences on your trip to Earth that are simply shows being put on for your benefit and characters walking around for your entertainment and experience.

If you are able to understand this now, while you are still on your trip rather than waiting until you get Home, then you can detach from what is happening around you. This would give you the benefit of experiencing your Earth trip without having the attachment to outcomes like you currently have. If you understand that what is happening around you is not *real* but a play being put on for your benefit, then you are able to let things be as they are, and not need them to be a certain way in order for you to be happy. It is so important for you to understand this that we may cover it again at a later time. We still suggest that you read this section over until it does make sense. Eventually you will come to understand what we are saying here.

# A Word or Two About the Word 'Caution'

Today we speak of love and the overabundance of fear that has been created in the world these days. When you are in a space of love, there is no room for fear. They do not mutually exist together; you are either in one place or the other.

Many times you have been given the challenge of choosing one or the other, but you have falsely chosen one while still believing you can exist in the other. To say that you exist in love, trust, and faith while still having 'caution' is an erroneous view, because the way that you view 'caution' is directly related to fear of an outcome. So this is not a possible combination.

We say again, while you are existing in one, you are not existing in the other. Energetically, caution is fear, but releasing the attachment to and judgment of outcomes can mitigate this. You use caution because you fear the outcome of an experience will not be as you desire and therefore be *bad* and by using caution you may prevent that outcome. The uncertainty you are feeling is the fear. Do you see? To have faith and jump off the cliff, or to step into the chasm with faith that the next step will rise before you as you move forward to take it, is an expression of Love and complete faith and not fearing the outcome of the experience. If you believe the step will be there but use caution just in case it is not, then it most likely will not be there because you are moving forward in the energy of fear, thus creating a self-fulfilling prophecy. Caution is an expression of fear, fear of the step not being there instead of knowing it will be.

To exist in Love is exclusive of caution. You use caution crossing the street because you fear a vehicle may hit you and fear the outcome of that experience. And as much as you fear being seriously hurt, you are even more afraid of dying because you are so attached to the physical form you currently reside in. So again, caution is an expression of fear. We are not saying that you should be running willy-nilly out into a street full of cars. We are saying that there is a difference between using caution because you are afraid of a possible outcome, and using caution with the full knowledge and understanding that any outcome from an experience is a neutral thing and does not require a judgment placed upon it. By understanding the difference we speak of, you are freeing yourselves from the fear aspect of caution. When no judgment of *good* or *bad* is placed on an outcome of an experience, then *caution* as you use this term, is not needed because you are not existing in fear of an outcome. Do you see the difference? Do you understand?

This may be difficult to separate out (caution equaling fear and caution without the fear aspect) because fear has become such an integral part of your existence. We hear you saying, "But I DO use caution without fear. I simply don't wish to be hurt or killed by a car". But we say to you, if you were to examine this closer, and objectively, you will see that you are indeed coming from a place of fear when you use caution because your world and your lives are inundated in expressions of fear and you currently are unable to separate the two. This is why we bring this topic to you now, to help you to understand that you can learn to allow caution to be an expression of neutrality and release yourselves from the judgment of outcomes. Learning to recognize fear in all its forms is an important lesson that we wish for you to learn, because with any amount of fear inhabiting your Being, you are disallowing the space that would be better served being filled with Light and Love. So, you must learn to recognize Fear in all of its different forms and no matter what mask it is wearing.

Think of it this way. When you see a 'Caution' sign, it has been posted to warn you of possible danger so that you will be forewarned to fear possibly being hurt. They want you to use caution because there may be harm involved if you do not, which is a way of placing fear of an outcome in you. But is also is an expression of fear for them as well, because they fear the outcome of someone hurting themselves and blaming them. Entire laws have been created to support this expression of fear, clearly stating which party would be 'at fault' if the proper PRE-cautions were not taken and there is a *bad* outcome. So now you have *cautions* and *pre-cautions*. Everyone is experiencing so much fear around things that may or may not happen that using caution was not enough and it now requires caution to get ahead of any other caution that may be deemed necessary. The propagation of 'caution' due to fear was planted long ago and has flowered as weeds in a yard where they have refused to be fully extinguished or from between the cracks in the sidewalks. At what point will you be willing to let go of the progression of evermore caution and understand that there is no *bad* outcome to any experience obfuscating the feeling that caution is necessary?

So many of you use the term 'caution' as a pretense for caring. Caring that involves fear is not at all helpful energetically. This is not done maliciously. Your friends and family urge you to use caution because they fear the outcome of what you are proposing to do or already doing, and you express caution to your loved ones because you fear the outcome of what they are proposing to do or already doing. We are back to the idea that having worry and concern for someone means you care, and if you do not then you do not care. This refers to our lesson of Detachment and allowing all events and people to be as they choose and how they need to be. By expressing caution, concern, and worry, a judgment is being placed on the outcome of an experience because of a fear of not doing it *right*, or again, that the outcome will not be what you want it to be. Thus, caution is used as an expression of fear.

The overuse of the term 'caution' in your languages is rampant. You see this word on signs, and flashing in bright lights, plastered on walls in bright red paint, or large symbols of skull and crossbones, or simply driving down a road. These 'caution' signs cause fear of having a *bad* outcome if you were to disregard them. There is no neutral meaning for the word as it is used in your society, and this also speaks to the control that is given to those that wield those signs to claim their power over you.

Fear is a tool that is used for control. This can be control from outside yourselves as well as from within from the

Ego-Self. On the personal side, when caution is felt necessary and it is being expressed from a feeling coming from inside of you, this is the Ego-Self using fear to control you. Not all power plays come from external sources; they also come from within. And they are the most successful when you are not aware of their machinations. The solution is as simple as first having the Awareness of those machinations, which we are now giving to you, and then paying attention and noticing when those machinations are being perpetrated against you. You DO have control of this. The only time you release that control is when you refuse to acknowledge the Awareness when it is given to you, and thusly fail to notice when these machinations are being used against you. It is always your choice, and we endeavor to help you to see and to understand that you do indeed have a choice whether to experience fear or not.

# A Message from Mother Gaia

In the passage of time we have seen many come and go who came among you to deliver these messages. They have not 'hit home' as we might have hoped. But we will never forsake you, for you are our family and we love you from the very depth of our Being. You are us and we are you. There is no separation, and only by taking hold of these lessons we offer will you come to full Realization of your Higher Self and your natural state of Being. We will never tire of helping you Awaken so that you may release yourselves from this cycle of reincarnation upon the very tired Mother Gaia. She is weary and in need of tending to her own needs and you are old enough to 'move out of the house' and take over your own care. In essence, you have graduated high school and must now decide if you are moving on to the next level of 'education', if you will be moving on to other experiences, or if perhaps you will be taking a 'gap year' before you continue your study.

Whichever choice you make is a correct one; there is no wrong choice. Mother Gaia has allowed you to 'live at home' for a period longer than was planned and it is now time for you to 'grow up and move out'. She will always be available to you energetically to support and love you as any mother would, but she is well overdue for a 'spa vacation' to fulfill her needs so that she can continue to give and be a part of this wonderful Universe. She is so tired and overused; she is depleted and has nothing left to give at this point. You will fulfill your time upon her surface and then will continue your chosen journey elsewhere. She will rest and recover and discover who she is unto herself once more. She has been a gracious Mother and sends you off with all the tools she has to offer to assist you on the next part of your journey.

She is excited for you and your upcoming experiences in new places but she is also excited to be advancing on her own journey. While she loves you all, she knows that she will have much more to give when she is able to replenish herself, her physical and energetic stores. Some, who have been with her since her time began so long ago, already know this. Others will come to full understanding only as they pass on to the next part of their journey and look back upon their experiences with Mother Gaia. Only then will they be able to energetically appreciate all that she has done and sacrificed for them. It is not that she requires this appreciation and understanding, but the flow of energy back and forth between you and Mother Gaia is very much enriched by this understanding. As one grows in understanding, compassion, and love, so all benefit from that understanding, compassion, and love. It is a true exchange of beautiful energy and will no longer be a one-sided experience for Gaia.

In this dimension of reality, she is held by her commitment to you. Once freed from that commitment upon the completion of the arrangement, she will be able to join her realities into an unfragmented experience. She has divided herself numerous times to fit the experience of the populations that lived in and on her and she is excited to coalesce back into the Being that she was initially intended to be - a part of the Multiverse as a whole Being rather than the fragmented pieces she has become to fulfill her contract with humanity.

This is her time. Her joy is overwhelming at the accomplishments humanity has made through her extended agreement with them. Mother Gaia is an immensely proud mother indeed, and wishes to express her love for the Starseeds that she welcomed to assist in humanity's development and growth. It has been quite the experience for all involved! She knows many of you are ready to go home for a rest. It has been a long stay for you as well, as you also extended your contracts with humanity, due to circumstances beyond your control, and have not been allowed to go home to rest between 'missions'. She understands the hardships you have endured and hopes that she was able to provide some sense of home for you while you have been here. She is not your home of origin, but it has been important for her to make you feel comfortable and welcome even during your homesickness. You are the ones that have helped her endure the extended contract because of your Unconditional Love, Compassion, and Appreciation for her as her own Energetic Being. Being 'seen' by you, as the sentient Being that she is, made a huge impact on her; she is forever grateful and wishes to express her love to you as well. She wishes to assure you, although you intuitively already know this, that the energy you shared with her for her healing has indeed been accepted with incredible gratefulness and helped her make it through this finishing cycle with humanity.

# The Eternal Moment of Now

So many times, you wander down an unknown road full of fear wondering what the future may hold for you. Your sole focus is on what lies ahead or what has happened in the past. When you are existing in past experiences or anticipating future events you are not living in the moment that you are currently in. When you are not focused on the now that you are currently in, then there is only the past and the future and that is not as good as it may sound. There is only the now moment - all else is illusion. Time is not linear; everything is now. You have created the illusion of time for your limited view to make more sense to you. But that does not make it any more real.

Linear time was also created to promote the idea of *fear*, and thus control. When you live in the past you *fear* you will make the same mistakes again. You may be full of regret, or guilt, wishing things had been different. Those are emotions that fall under the *fear* category. When you live fixated on the future, you are worried what is yet to be will not be what you desire it to be. Worry is another emotion that falls under the *fear* category. Only by existing in each moment as it arrives are you able to choose not to *fear*, and as you do this you are able to move forward without guilt or regrets and without worry for a future yet to be. If every moment is now, then each moment you are making the choice to exist in *fear* or to exist in *love*.

Why would you live in fear if you have a choice? First of all, because you are not aware that you have a choice. You have been conditioned over many eons to submit to fear so that others have control over you, so that your emotions can feed them energetically. Those that presented themselves as gods, and allowed you to believe it, lured you into accepting this control. In your experience of Duality, which was a request for an experience and granted by the One Infinite Creator, you left yourselves vulnerable to their influence. The Creator, in all his loving Wisdom, allowed this requested experience but has never left your side. In your perception of separation while experiencing humanity on the Earth, you feel as though you have been deserted to your Fate. But we tell you this is not so. We are always with you and always respond to your requests for assistance. We do so to the best of our ability, while still honoring your Free Will to have this experience to its fullest.

Secondly, this was allowed to happen as an experience of Duality. Duality meant experiencing love, joy, elation as well as fear, worry, and angst - both sides of the spectrum. You are receiving the experience you desired. You disbelieve this because you ask yourself, "Why would I do this to myself? Why would I voluntarily choose to experience pain, fear, longing, all of these fear-based emotions?" It seems inconceivable to you now that you would have made such a choice. But if you were able to put yourself back into the feeling of wonder at being offered a chance to experience the Earth as an inhabitant, it would make sense to you.

We have used this analogy before: it is as if you were told you could take a trip to the happiest place on Earth and you were ecstatic about going on all the rides and trying all the different foods and drinks available there, all the new experiences that were not available anywhere else. Duality offers a compare and contrast situation that is only available here. That is why it is such a desirable place to be allowed to incarnate.

Please understand, we do know the difficulties you experience here; we do not wish to take away from that. But you must understand that it is your choice to look outside of yourself and understand that you did choose this experience for yourself. This is a part of the lessons given regarding taking your power back. You make yourself stronger by objectively looking at a situation and not turning away from the pain of the experiences or lulling yourself to sleep feeling sorry for yourself as a victim. You are only a victim when you turn away and thus allow the situation power over you. You are only a victim if you allow yourself to be. If you turn and face this situation, and seek the deeper understanding that comes from finding your True Self, the Spiritual Being you actually are, excited by the opportunity to have this experience here, then you would be able to look at the situation differently and thus change the outlook you currently hold regarding your time here on Earth. You wish yourself elsewhere, and then when you are elsewhere in Spirit, you understand the opportunity that you cut short.

The time for this cycle is now over. We wish you to reach this understanding before you return to Spirit because this will be the last go round on this merry-go-round and we wish to see you reach all the goals you have set for yourself while you are still here, as you wished to do. The understanding of the gift you were granted by being given this incarnation on the Earth plane must be realized, but that understanding is only achieved by seeking out and knowing your True Self, your True Nature. Otherwise you are lost in the illusion of the physical body and will never be able to see this experience from the perspective of your Higher Self.

How difficult is it to move beyond the illusion of the physical body? We have incarnated and are incarnated among you at this time so that we can understand the difficulties of your taking this physical form. Many teachers over the eons have incarnated among you to show you the way home, but you have not been ready - as you are now. You are on the cusp of a great event that will change things forever. The only way through this event will be by passing through the eye of the needle. There will be no going around it. You are either through the center or you are moving on to your next learning experience where you will be given the chance once more to learn what you desired but did not accomplish on the Earth during your sojourn here.

This is meant as encouragement to continue to seek out and reach for your goals. There is no judgment at all placed on where any soul chooses to reside or what path they choose to follow. That is the beauty of Unconditional Love. You are loved by the One Infinite Creator, no matter your choices because you are never separate. As you experience, so does all of creation along with you. All is perfect in every choice. There are no mistakes because each decision and choice simply leads to an experience to be had. The Creator only desires what you desire for yourselves and revels in your joy, while having complete and total compassion for the pain that you feel from your perceived separation while in this most challenging form you have chosen. We assure you, you may feel separated from the One Infinite Creator while in human form, but the Creator is still a spark inside you, even if you are currently unable to acknowledge it.

Do not give up on your search for understanding. The way home is found by entering your Heart Center, for that is the magical portal that you are seeking. It has been within you all the time. So, stop searching outside yourself for the answers to returning home. Turn inside, where the answers truly lie, and reconnect with your True Higher Essence and the One Infinite Creator that all life has sprung forth from. You have been long awaited. We welcome you home with open arms as you take the first steps on the path that returns you home and to complete awakening to the circumstances of your recent journey.

# The Time has Come to Choose a Polarity

As we began this journey so very long ago, little was known of the Kingdom of Heaven. This information was brought to you in the form of a human who shared the wisdom of the ages with you. And then another came, and then another, and another. So many times, this message was brought to you, but it has always been misinterpreted by those who would use the information to cause confusion and turn the words to their advantage, to use for nefarious purposes. The time for this to be allowed has passed; this tactic will no longer be tolerated by those that have been incarnated here to help you, as well as those that are still in the Realm beyond your mortal eyes' ability to see.

This is the time foretold of many times, but it is not the way those who turn the purpose of the words towards Service-to-Self purposes think it will be. Those that use these tidings to propagate fear among all of humanity will no longer be allowed to twist the meaning of these words towards their purpose of control. So, we have returned to speak these words again to you without the possibility of them being misconstrued and twisted again.

This is the time that in your hearts of hearts you have dreamed and longed for. For some it will mean moving on to a different planet where the 'New Earth', as it is currently being called, will be available to host the portion of humanity that is ready to move on to learn about Collective Consciousness of the 4th Density Service-to-Others Polarity. This New Earth is Utopia, the Garden of Eden, the Shangri-La, the perfect world that you have dreamed of inhabiting. There will be no 3rd Density at all on this New Earth. You will no longer need to try to exist in the in-between of 3rd and 4th Density. You who have shown that you have firmly chosen Service-to-Others Polarity will be moving to a new location to pursue the Spiritual Growth that this opportunity will allow.

Do not be fooled into believing that you will travel there on physical ships of light. You are not meant to travel to the New Earth in this fashion. Your Earth 3rd Density bodies were not meant to exist on planets other than the Earth, where the gravity field is much denser than on other planets, including the planet that will become your new host.

Think outside the box. You have not been able to perceive that your move to 4th Density would require an actual move to a different physical location. When the 'New Earth' was referred to you only thought it was called that because everything will change and become new. In one respect that has some truth to it. Your Mother Gaia is indeed changing physically and progressing on her evolution even as humanity does. She will no longer be habitable by humanity, or anything but the lowest Densities, for an extended period of time as she goes through her rest and recovery. Therefore, when we refer to the 'New Earth', we literally mean a new planet that is yet to be named. The naming of your new home will be done through the Collective Consciousness of the new inhabitants.

It is very beautiful there and will have none of the experiences you have come to associate with being in physical form upon the Earth. The experience of Duality will no longer be required, as you have completed that experience to your satisfaction while on Mother Gaia. You will recognize all others as parts of yourself being expressed in different shapes and forms, for you will have the understanding that living in Unity Consciousness provides. You will understand and live the truth of those words at last and to their fullest. You will not be able to hurt yourself because you will have the understanding that by doing so you are also hurting others. Neither will you be able to hurt others because you will fully understand that by hurting others you are also hurting yourself, because you are experiencing Unity Consciousness. There will be no desire to take advantage of others for personal gain, and no need to be 'cautious' in case others try to take advantage of you, because on the New Earth you experience Unity Consciousness. The New Earth will be everything you dreamed of and longed for and it is now your destiny.

Those of you that have not yet chosen their Polarity at the time of the Harvest Event, as it is called, will be given the opportunity to once again incarnate on a planet that has offered to host a 3rd Density experience for you. This is a most gracious gift being given to humanity. As you see from living on Mother Gaia, the experience can definitely have a serious toll paid by the sentient planet offering itself for the sake of humanity's growth. And as in the case of

Mother Gaia, who graciously allowed humanity's experience to extend long past what was advisable in order to be of Service-to-Others, this is always a possibility when a sentient planet takes on this endeavor. This planet Being is lovingly giving what can seem like a blink of an eye, or a speck of dust in the eye if not completed in a timely fashion, in order to host you. This task is not taken on lightly. It is hoped that by experiencing 3$^{rd}$ Density on a new planet with a different set of circumstances than occurred on the Earth, that this round of 3$^{rd}$ Density work will be completed in the usual time allotted for such endeavors. It will not be the experience that those moving on to 4$^{th}$ Density Service-to-Others Polarity will have, however it will be different than what you are currently experiencing.

If you are not yet moving on to the 4$^{th}$ Density Positive Polarity experience, it does not mean you have failed at anything. Release your limiting human concepts of success and failure when you consider where you may be going. As long as you are of the Service-to-Others Polarity a majority of the time, you will be moving on to the 4$^{th}$ Density Positive experience. However, you are loved and valued by the Creator even if you have not settled yet on Service-to-Others or Service-to-Self Polarity. Since you have not settled on one or the other, you are simply not yet ready to move on to the next level of experiencing. Here is an analogy of this situation. In school, those in the 3$^{rd}$ grade who passed all the tests and have an understanding of all the materials presented in that classroom show that they are ready to move on to the next classroom to learn the material there. This would be like moving on to 4$^{th}$ Density Positive Polarity. Those that have not shown an understanding of the material presented in the 3<sup>rd</sup> grade must repeat the experience, which is for their benefit. They would be those going to another 3<sup>rd</sup> Density planet to continue learning 3<sup>rd</sup> Density material Again we say, release the human need to place judgments of *good*, *bad*, *failure* and *success* to these circumstances. It is only your human perceptions of these terms that make them true for you, but in reality they are simply an illusion that you have created for reasons we have gone into previously. Release these judgments. Fully understand and accept when we tell you - there is absolutely no judgment by the Creator, (or any but your human-selves), placed on you if you are not yet ready to advance to the next classroom. You are simply being given every opportunity to be successful in experiences that lead you back to your full unity with the Creator. The path and time frame you choose to achieve that goal is completely up to you and is always honored with complete Unconditional Love, Unconditional Forgiveness, and Unconditional Non-Judgment. Those moving to the new 3<sup>rd</sup> Density experience will also be leaving their physical Earth bodies behind, as they are not meant for that new home either. Again, the gravity on Mother Earth is much denser than the planet that will be hosting the new 3<sup>rd</sup> Density experience.

Now, for those that are of firm Service-to-Self Polarity, they will be reaping what they have sown. They have used their Free Will to harm others for personal gain and they will also be moving on to new experiences in different locations. As we have said, all will be leaving Mother Gaia at the appointed time and moving on to different locations. Those that are of Service-to-Self Polarity have been given the same opportunities that all souls have, and by their choices have created much Karmic debt that is due for payment. They will be moving on to experience what they themselves have wrought upon many souls in their time on Mother Gaia. They have allowed themselves to be influenced by the darker souls that have had influence upon the Earth for many millennia, and truly what you sow you shall reap.

There is no judgment placed by the Creator on these darker souls or those that have submitted to their influences. It is simply another facet to the experiences to be had in the Universes. This is why it is so very important to understand what we are teaching about true Unconditional Love, Forgiveness, and Non-Judgment. Unless you release your human perceptions of placing conditions on love, being unable to forgive yourself or others, and judging yourself and others, you will never be able to understand the concepts we are giving you of the Creators deep felt Unconditional Love, Forgiveness, and Non-Judgment of these darker souls and those who choose to live by their example and influence.

Those of Service-to-Self Polarity will be moving on to an excruciating experience of slavery to those they have followed who will claim them for their own purposes once again. In your compassion and empathy for others you feel deeply for their plight, but do not lose yourself in their experience believing that you can change their minds before it is too late. While it may be true in some cases that they are still able to turn things around for themselves, it is their responsibility to seek out and complete that change, not yours. You would be of more assistance to those that have not yet decided on which Polarity they believe in, but do not create entanglement with them. You are less likely to be of assistance if you are dragged into the quicksand alongside them. Therefore, hold your auric space at all times, and guide them out by extending a branch and lifting them to where you are rather than meeting them down in the quicksand and trying to pull the both of you up. Does this make sense?

All paths will meet up eventually and lead to the same place: back to the full unity with the Creator. The only difference is the experience and the time it will take for those of differing Polarities. There is no need to place judgment on the path that another chooses for this reason. How they wish to travel to the same destination as everyone else is by preference and a choice of which experience is desired. If someone wishes to travel by train rather than plane, the only difference is how he/she is traveling; both modes of travel are just as valid and useful. Do not allow yourselves to fall into the trap of judging another's preferred mode of travel or path based on what you prefer. Opinions are judgments. The saying goes, "Everyone has an opinion", but we are here to tell you that you do not need to. In fact, it is much healthier for you if you do not have one, because, once again, the goal is Unconditional Love, Forgiveness, and Non-Judgment. By having an opinion about those that have chosen to follow the darker soul's experience, you are judging them and their chosen path and thereby not following or attaining the goals that have been set for you to achieve for advancement. Do you see the folly, and how easily it is to fall into judgment?

You must first heal and help yourselves before you can help others. You must first recognize in yourselves the human failings of placing conditions on your love, the inability and unwillingness to forgive yourself and others, and judging yourself and others in any degree. You must be willing to change these behaviors in and for yourself before you can help others to do the same. It is important to understand this so that you may consciously choose to make the necessary changes. As they say on airplanes, if the mask drops you must first put yours on before trying to help others. You are unable to help others unless you help yourself first in this scenario. If you passed out, you would be unable to help those who might need your help. It is so clear when expressed in this way, yet you are all conditioned to think yourself (or others) selfish if you help yourself first, or take care of yourself before reaching out to help others. Yet when you think of this analogy of the speech they give on planes, you are able to see the logic behind helping yourself first. It is no different in any other circumstance. We ask you to see and understand this because while it does apply now, it will become even more important as the time approaches for the coming Harvest Event.

The most important thing to take away from this chapter is the understanding of how important it is to choose and to live a life of Service-to-Others Polarity. Even if it is a steady fifty one percent, that is still a majority of the time and shows the Universe your intention of being Service-to-Others Polarity. Your desire to stand firmly on that path will lead you to the only destination there is for any path - back to the One Infinite Creator. However, the Service-to-Others path will allow you to travel there via the New Earth and a 4th Density Positive Polarity experience.

# Faith

Many times, humans fall back on what they like to call *faith* because that is what they were taught in parochial schools or in the religious institutions that they grew up in. Faith is a term used loosely by humans to mean many things. Mostly it is used to replace the word hope, as in "I have faith that the Lord will bring us what we need", or "I have faith that everything will turn out as it should". This is a very shallow meaning and is not the meaning of the word when we speak of it to you. When we use the word Faith it has such a deeper meaning than you currently understand. That is why we wish to take this opportunity to define it for you, expressing the True Essence behind the meaning of the word.

Faith, by our definition when we speak to you, is a way of truly expressing the deep-seated knowingness of the One Infinite Creator. It is still a weak term to explain the depth of understanding and knowingness, contained in your soul memory, of the secrets of the Universes. The word Faith has come to be associated with a non-committed acceptance of the truths of the meanings of the Universes, kept in your soul memories for retrieval upon your readiness for the full knowledge. Meaning you hope what you intuitively know is true, but you are not willing to commit to the statement of intent of this, neither to yourself nor to others.

How difficult it is to exist in such a state! You long to remember your full self, and yet have settled for acknowledging only what you hope you intuitively know to be true is indeed true. Hence when you say you must see to believe you will in fact never see, because faith, as you refer to it, is a flimsy commitment to the truth. We tell you now - you must first believe in order to see. As quantum mechanics has shown, what you look at is only there when you look at it; if you must see it before you look at it then you will never see it. Do you understand? This is why you must give up *faith* that you will see something so that you can believe in it. You must first believe in it so that when you look you will see it.

And this brings up our definition of Faith. The real meaning of Faith is following your knowingness with no proof to support your knowingness. When you are able to trust your innate knowingness, then you do not require proof and you do not feel it necessary to convince others of the truth of your knowingness. Each will find their own knowingness in their own time, and whether they are convinced in the validity of yours or not is irrelevant to the Faith you have in your own knowingness. By this definition Faith is a conviction, not a hope. Do you see the difference we speak of? It is a big difference, and the difference matters.

The unwavering conviction of the Faith we speak of is not a fanatical thing either. There are those who twist the meaning to their advantage, who claim their Faith is a conviction that 'God' stands behind. They use it as a weapon against others to procure wealth, fame, and notoriety for themselves and to gain followers. This is a corrupted version of the definition that we speak of. This provides an opportunity for you to practice Discernment. If someone is trying to convince you that their faith is strong and that you must have the same faith as they do, then that is a clue that they are corrupting the true meaning we give you of Faith and you would be wise to move in the opposite direction.

Such opportunities do come up for a reason though. This would be a learning example, a chance to practice Discernment and to learn to trust your own knowingness and not bow to another's. The difficulty you find in not blindly following others has been programmed into you many eons ago. You were trained to give up your power to others and to follow blindly when another expresses conviction in their faith, in their knowingness of the 'right' way to go. This is a corrupted version of the shepherd and his flock. While the shepherd leads benevolently, guiding and caring for his sheep out of love for their wellbeing, the corrupted version has been twisted so that humanity would follow blindly, as slavery, to the one that leads them.

We bring this Awareness to you because this corrupted version has been used successfully for so long that humanity is not aware of themselves being the sheep, but fancy themselves the lions that know what they are doing and are willing to go after what they want. The deception has been so successful that humanity is not even aware that they are indeed the sheep. The conviction of those that have corrupted the true definition of Faith have managed to guide you while letting you believe that it is all your idea when you are doing what they wish you to do.

No one likes to hear the painful truth that they have given over their personal strength and power to others. Yet it is only through Awareness that you can make a change. And it is you yourself that must make the change; no one can do the work for you. You must first become Aware of the situation, (which is what we are bringing to you here in our messages), and then consciously choose to recognize where and how you have given over your power and allowed the convictions of others to override your own innate knowingness. Once you do these things, then the hold over you is lost. Understand that this will make those that seek to control you in this way angry. However, if you are following the tools that we are giving you for your Spiritual advancement then you will understand that there truly is nothing to fear at all from this. You will be able to understand that even the deepest fear from going against the 'norm', and breaking away from the corrupted version of a flock is no longer necessary.

When you fully integrate and understand what we are teaching you, you remember that this is only one life, one experience among millions that you will have. When your current physical form no longer exists, your true Soul Essence continues on to its next experience. Once you integrate this understanding, which speaks to humanity's deepest darkest fear of all, then you realize there is no reason to be afraid of anything at all. You understand that there is nothing lost from standing up for yourself and taking your power back. There is nothing to be lost from detaching from the convictions of others and following your own innate Knowingness, which gives you the Faith to maneuver through this experience of 3rd Density humanity on Mother Gaia. You are stronger than you know; you just need a little help remembering that fact and the encouragement and support to follow your own path and not the path someone else would lead you down.

We hear you thinking, "I only follow someone because their conviction coincides with my conviction". And we tell you again, that you feel that way because you are being coaxed to believe. The choice to follow this 'shepherd' is yours. You really are convinced this is your own idea. But we tell you this is not so, because they are meeting you on a playing field of fear, in whatever guise they choose to clothe that in, and you feel compelled to follow them because you think they believe as you do. In truth, they have their own agenda and they are using that conviction to control you, all the while encouraging you to believe it was your idea. Look at the 'man' behind the curtain, not the face that is presented before you. Again, this is the importance that we speak of in learning to live from your Heart Center so that you may use your Intuition and Discernment to flush out these imposters that would control you.

Live not by Faith alone, but by Discernment and Love of Life and All That Is to find the completeness in yourself that you are seeking. Long has been the time since you were separated, and it is as if you were waking from a long, deep slumber. You are still a little drowsy from your long sleep, but as the cobwebs clear from your mind and you come to full Awakening you will comprehend all. All will return to you if you choose to focus on waking up. Now is the time to clear the sleep away and fully remember what was happening before you began your slumber. It is time to return to the tasks you began long ago and have yet to complete. Now is the time.

# Unconditional Love, Forgiveness, and Non-Judgment

There is more than one type of Love. There are infinitesimal expressions of Love that you have not even conceived of yet. Your most well-known definition of Love is when you are referring to romantic love. We tell you, this type of love pales in comparison to the deeper understanding of Love. You are deeply entrenched in this physical experience you are having, and as such feel that romantic love is the best thing going because that is the most tangible form of love that you remember experiencing. It feels this way because it is a pale reminder of the deeper knowledge of an all-encompassing Love that resides in your Soul Memory.

There is a Love so deep that it is incomprehensible in your current physical form. You have glimpses of it through the act of making love and when you use psychedelic substances that release you, for a time, from the confines of your physical form. But even those are but reminders, a mere sip from the cup, of the full meaning and experience of Love.

In choosing to have this human experience you understood that many things would be given up for a time, one of them being the constant awareness of the Love from the One Infinite Creator. It is not that the constant flow of Love is not there, but that your awareness of it is affected. This can be changed while you are still in human form. There is nothing saying that you cannot regain this experience of the constant Unconditional Love from the One Infinite Creator while you are still in physical form. If you put forth the effort and use the tools and knowledge we are giving you here, this can be achieved.

There is no time limit set for this task. As long as you have set your goal and steadily work towards its completion then you are on your way. You have set up opportunities along the way to remind you that this was a goal that you wished to achieve. For example, seeing this book, picking it up and feeling connected to it before you even read it is one such failsafe switch that you set for yourself. Do not fret! You have given yourself many opportunities to help you remember your True Self, and if you miss one there will always be another. Do not worry that you may have missed something. Just continue, in the moment you are in, to do what feels like the correct thing to be doing. As you learn to exist in your Heart Center, it becomes easier to hear the guidance being given to you by your Higher Self and your Guides in order to make that connection. This is an important reason to do the homework we assign you so that you may achieve this ability to exist in your Heart Center.

What truth do you seek that Love cannot answer? None! There is none! Love truly is the answer to everything. All answers to all questions are found there, in Unconditional Love. It is the creation of the Mother/Father Creator and is the ultimate gift to give and to receive. There is no higher gift to be attained or achieved. Only when you know this, really KNOW this, will you be set free. You turn away from this knowledge because it is so much more than you can seem to bear in your current form. But we tell you: you do not need to fear what you will see by turning to face this incredible gift that is Unconditional Love. And we tell you: you cannot gift it to others until you are able to gift it to yourself. Only in giving Unconditional Love to yourself do you fully comprehend the power that lies within the gift. Only by gifting it to yourself can you fully comprehend and fully gift this Unconditional Love to others. For in gifting it to yourself first, you are able to understand the deepest form of acceptance and understanding available to you in physical form. Only by gifting it to yourself can you understand the impact it has on others. It is life changing and not something to be missed.

In order to be able to gift yourself with Unconditional Love and then gift it to others, you must first be willing to experience Non-Judgment. We speak of even the smallest of 'opinions' that are based on what you were taught are *right* or *wrong*, *good* or *bad*, because this is where judgment stems from. If you are not able to let go of those concepts, then you will be unable to achieve this very important factor of Non-Judgment, for yourself and for others. Only when you are able to let go of judgment, even in the smallest forms, can you move on to achieve Unconditional Love. For without Non-Judgment you will never reach true Unconditional Love.

If you were to pay attention to your thoughts and see how many times you actually make a judgment about someone or what they're doing, you would be very surprised. It has become such an ingrained habit that you do not even realize you are doing it. For instance, you pull into a parking lot and look for a parking space and a car comes down the aisle in the wrong direction. Do you not place judgment on how that person is doing it *wrong*? When someone lets an elevator door close before you reach it, do you not judge that person as being inconsiderate for not noticing you approaching and holding the door open for you? Need we go on with further examples? We think not. It is so important to pay attention to circumstances such as these and see that even in those small moments you are placing judgments. Yes! Even the smallest of judgments will keep you from the ultimate goal of Unconditional Love, because if you are doing it for these smallest of incidents, you are doing it for the bigger incidents as well. The bigger incidents may be easier to catch, but the smaller ones are more significant for the very fact that they are harder to notice. ALL judgment, big and small, must go in order to truly experience and exist in the space of Unconditional Love.

Now it is important to remember Unconditional Forgiveness, for yourselves and others. When you go through the process of recognizing how often you actually place judgments on yourself or others, you must be willing to give Unconditional Forgiveness. When you recognize that you do not have to judge others for something you perceived they have done to you, then you are able to jump directly to Unconditional Forgiveness. You may do something with the best of intentions, but the outcome is not what you desired. Once you recognize that there is no need to judge yourself for it, you can go directly to Unconditional Forgiveness for yourself. Unconditional Forgiveness is a gift you must give yourself, as well as to others.

How important these three concepts are! Hopefully you

are able to see now how they interact. You cannot have one without the others. It takes all three to have all three because they are directly intertwined together. These concepts of Unconditional Love, Forgiveness, and Non-Judgment are the cornerstone of building a solid foundation to build your Spirituality upon. These are the first basic tools to achieve and master in order to reach the higher levels of Spirituality that lead you back to your True Essence.

Do not skip steps. We give you each for a reason and will hold you to learning them all so that you may incorporate them and accurately pass them on to those whom you will be teaching in kind. Even if you do not hold formal classes in Spirituality, you are a teacher to all around you by living what you learn. It is as a pebble thrown into a calm lake, which causes a ripple effect that echoes out to all the edges of the lake. But in this case, there is no edge to the lake because energy has no end. It goes out and repeats back to you, hence the saying "What you put out there comes back to you tenfold." The energy of the ripple will go out, affect others who will amplify the signal, and eventually return to you. This is a Universal Truth, and why what you choose to 'put out there' really does make a difference, even if you are currently unable to view it or experience it.

So, we implore you. Learn these tools. Incorporate them into your life and live by them and your world will change to be more of what you desire it to be. Even if not everyone does this, your world changes because your perception of it changes. Do you understand? So do not worry about what others are doing or not doing; all that matters is what you are doing. All it takes for your world to change is you changing your own perception.

# More than Dreaming

Many of you are having strange dreams as of late. Do you wonder why this is? There is so much teaching going on during your sleep, more now than ever. It is important to try to consciously take in these lessons at this time. They have always been taken in by your sub-conscious, and they still are, but the time has come to integrate them into your conscious mind as well.

Dreams have always been a way for you to work out what was happening in your daily waking life, but they are also reminders of days past. For those who do not believe in past lives, it doesn't mean they do not exist; it just means that you do not remember them. They are as real as the day you are having today, and in fact are occurring today. This is where you need to let go of the concept of linear time; otherwise you will never be able to comprehend the truth we speak of your 'previous' lives.

You perceive them as 'past' or 'previous' lives, but really neither word is correct. For all intents and purposes, you are experiencing them all at the same time. This goes back to our lesson about the water cooler. If you remember, the pitcher that draws from the water cooler is poured into a glass, but it is also poured into more than one glass. Each glass filled is another expression of your Soul having an experience. It is not one glass that keeps being filled over and over again; the water in the glass does not go anywhere so you cannot keep refilling the same glass. Therefore, multiple glasses are filled at the same time. That means that your Soul Essence is filling many different 'glasses' and having many different experiences at the same time. Do you see? Does this analogy help you to understand what we mean about linear time being an illusion and that you are actually having multiple experiences at the same time?

Just because you currently do not remember all the other parts of yourself does not mean they do not exist; it just means you do not remember them currently. And that is not to say that those other parts of yourself do not remember you in your current form and experience. As we have said before, this human experience on the Earth was a chosen experience by each of you for your own reasons, and part of that experience involved forgetting yourself, meaning all parts of yourself were forgotten.

An important part of this Ascension process is remembering all parts of yourself, seeing through the illusion of linear time so that you can grasp the concept of your True Higher Self. If you continue to grasp tightly to your human 3$^{rd}$ Density experiences and deny any other experiences, you will be unable to reconnect with all the parts of yourself that are currently having experiences in other times and other dimensions. You will be unable to grasp the vastness of your True Soul Self in all its wonder and glory. We know this may be a lot to ask, to wrap your minds around such a vast experience, but as you consider our analogy you will begin to let go of the human created concept of time and have an understanding of what we are explaining to you.

There is much to be gained from your understanding of this matter we teach because you are still able to contact and connect with these other pieces of yourself that are in other places and times if you allow yourself to. You may not be able to do so with those parts of you that are currently having Earth experiences in different time periods where they are also lost in the concept of linear time and do not have a belief system that supports the concept of having other lives other than the one they are experiencing. But those parts of you that are having experiences in places other than the Earth plane have the awareness of this truth and are ready and waiting to connect with you. Some have already done this. You may see channeling sessions on one of the social media platforms, or alternative TV shows where those that are connected with other parts of themselves in other places are gifting that knowledge to others. Their other selves are sharing important information for humanity's advancement because those other selves did not get lost in the veil of forgetfulness that humanity on Earth did. Therefore, they still remember the Universal Truths and are connecting with the piece of themselves having this Earth based incarnation to help themselves and all who will listen to what they have to say.

We know this is a big leap for some of you to make, while for others this is a validation of knowing that you have had for a while. Dreams can help you to integrate this information, which is why we encourage listeners to have a journal and a writing utensil next to their bed to be able to write their dreams down upon waking. Not only can you look back at it later, but you will also recall more of a dream as you are writing it down.

Some dreams may be your unconscious expressing itself about the day's events, but more and more we are using dreams to help teach you the lessons you need to learn, teach you the things you need to remember. And sometimes they are a bleed through of the experiences one of your other Soul-Selves is having. You may notice a feeling of incredible realness to a dream because this is a connection to your other Self and experiencing of a piece of the reality through the other Self's experience. When you wake up and feel that remembering the dream is like remembering what you did yesterday, it is a good indication that you have been connecting with your other Self. They also experience this and have the same experience you do. Those in the dreams that you recognize as someone you know in your waking life are a part of the soul group that you incarnate with over and over. While they may look different in the dream, you know they are the same person in your waking life, and they are also with your other Self, having that experience.

What we ask you to work on is to bring the Awareness and the connection you have in your dreams to your waking life. Some of you are saying, "But I never remember my dreams." This does not mean you are not having them. You are just not remembering them, and you can change that. There are stones and crystals that can be of service in this area. Hold them prior to lying down in bed and place an intention to remember your dream experiences. Then place the stone on the nightstand beside you. Holding the stone and stating your intent will program the energy of the stone to assist you in the task you are requesting. There are a number of stones that can offer this assistance and we ask you to practice your intuition in connecting with the one that resonates with you.

Sometimes it is sub-conscious fear of the dream experience that keeps you from fully participating in the dream teaching and learning experiences. You may say, "I am not afraid to remember my dreams. They are only dreams after all." But we tell you they are more than what you think, and at some point you had what you call a 'nightmare' and never wanted to remember your dream experiences again. For this we suggest something for all to do as a daily ritual. Before going to sleep, sit comfortably, close your eyes, and ground yourself deep into Mother Gaia. A good way to picture this is to see tree roots coming from you and going deep down into Mother Gaia. (You can picture in your mind whatever works best for you, but if you do not already have a good visual for grounding you can start with tree roots.) Then picture a waterfall of beautiful comforting white light shining down from the Creator and washing through your body while you ask for all the energy you have absorbed from others to wash out, through your grounding, into Mother Gaia. Then ask to wash out any stagnant energy of your own that is ready to be released through your grounding and into Mother Gaia. Then ask for assistance in 'holding your space', and visualize a bright bubble of healthy energy around you where you can be assisted in holding a higher vibrational light. Then ask for your aura to be strengthened and any damage to it be healed. Picture white and gold light coming down on top of the bubble around you and flowing down the sides like chocolate would flow over a round candy, coating it. Then ask your Guides, Angels, Ancestors, whomever you feel is with you and assisting you, to help you with everything they can. This part is as important as the rest because Free Will does place restrictions on when we can step in. By asking us daily to assist with everything we can, you are using your Free Will to allow us to step in when we see there is something that we can help with. In that way we are honoring your Free Will and not overriding it.

Whether you have difficulty remembering dreams or not, we recommend these steps be added to your daily routine, preferably as a way to start your day, but it can be done anytime and multiple times a day. These steps are also helpful when in stressful situations, to help bring calm and peace and bring you back to your Heart Center. This brings you to the place that meditation does. In fact this is a good way to begin a meditation, to help get you into that calm, Heart Centered space.

By washing yourself in a waterfall of light and sending it through your grounding to Mother Gaia, you wash out of your physical and etheric bodies any old stagnant energy, and any new energies you have absorbed. This is important because these stagnant energies, when left to fester, become physical pain and illness when they transfer from the etheric body to the physical body. When this stagnant energy remains for too long, it can manifest physical symptoms for which no explanation can be found.

These steps can take as long as you want. If you are short on time, it only takes a few minutes to close your eyes and go through each step. If you have more time and want to enjoy the wonderful feeling these steps bring, then you can draw it out longer. It is up to you. Either way we recommend incorporating these steps into your daily life.

## *Your Mission*

The lesson we wish to give today is threefold. Thrice the intricacy of explanation on our part, but we will deliver it with as much simplicity as possible. It is not that you are incapable of understanding the lesson we give to you, it is just that your human brain gets in the way of allowing your Spirit to remember itself. This is why we encourage each and every one to follow our recommendation of incorporating a meditation practice. If you follow the lesson we give regarding meditation and you learn to live from your Heart Center, then you are better able to grasp the more advanced concepts we give to you. Your Heart Center is the part of you that will remember and understand what we are saying to you, whereas your mind never will. If you are following this advice, we ask that you go now into your Heart Center before you continue reading.

Each person has come to this planet with a mission: a mission known only to you and the Soul Group that is working with you. This Soul Group knows the plans that you made for yourself and they help you fulfill those plans, some by playing roles in your life and some by staying behind in Spirit form to guide you along your chosen path. You are doing the same for them in different capacities as well while in all your different incarnations, but also through your Higher Self in the Spirit Realm. As we have spoken before, we all exist in more than one form at a time (all stemming from your Higher Self) and complete many tasks at the same time, while all the pieces of the whole take in the experiences and the lessons learned by all the fractal pieces.

Without fully understanding the whys of every little thing, you must accept that you are one small tiny piece of a whole so large it is difficult for you to comprehend in your current limited human form. If you have been doing the work on yourself that we suggested then you are beginning to sense the depth of what you have forgotten. Nothing that we tell you is new to you; you have simply forgotten. Our goal is to help you to remember. A big part of the work that we are asking you to do is to re-member yourself, to bring all the scattered pieces back together again while you are still in this human form. We refer to the pieces that have scattered and been ignored and denied by you due to the traumas experienced throughout your incarnations on the Earth. Traumas that are not dealt with when they occur, or before you leave an incarnation, will return with you to be resolved. Energy that is created in the physical must be resolved while in the physical, and you bring many unresolved traumas back with you each time that you incarnate. This is why Past Life Therapy is so important. Just as you, in this lifetime, would see a counselor after suffering a trauma to help you work through what happened, so too does an Intuitive Past Life Therapist help you resolve traumas that were not dealt with in past lives. The Past Life Therapist is only a facilitator; it is you who must do the real work to release the energy of these traumas. It also takes time to work through these energies, like peeling the layers from an onion as you reveal deeper and deeper issues related to the trauma. As you reveal each layer and heal and forgive yourself, you bring the pieces of yourself back to you. You are allowing yourself to be set free from the amnesia that held you hostage every time you returned to the Earth plane. It has been allowed to continue thus for a very long time, but the time has come, as we've previously stated, for you to free yourself of that yoke and step away from that self-imprisonment for good.

Another important matter to bring up is your tendency towards resentment. Resentment will only hold you back from progressing to the next desired level. When you were told of the occurrences that have been holding you back from your progress for so long, it created a deep-seated resentment in you. You feel justified in feeling this way since you feel a great injustice has been perpetrated against you. This again falls back to Awareness – being aware that you are feeling this resentment, acknowledging its presence, and then releasing it through the understanding that it is not necessary. Everything has happened for a reason, even if you do not understand. You do not need to understand to recognize the feeling and to let it go. Remember, this feeling would fall under the Fear Emotion and as such can only harm *you*, no other. If you are not letting this emotion go, then you are not living in Unconditional Love, Forgiveness and Non-Judgment. If you choose to hold on to the resentment, *you* are now the one holding yourself back. Do you see?

And yet another reason to study the material we are offering to you is the opportunity it gives you to live by the code of Unconditional Love, Forgiveness and Non-Judgment that the One Infinite Creator requires of you. This is the only true path back to yourself. The darkness that you have existed in for so long is lifting. Now it is up to you to travel to the pre-ordained location to meet up with your True Self so that you may combine your energy once more. No longer must you live separated from your True Higher Self. The time for the experience of Separation is over; it is complete. It has been agreed upon that your experience shall now move on to the next level with no further delays. However, this is not a magical pill that you can take to achieve this transformation; you must do the work yourself. Each and every one of you is responsible for your own Ascension process and must take responsibility for getting yourself prepared. There are many, here in physical form and in Spirit, to help you and guide you, but they cannot do the work for you. It must be your choice and your work to remember what you have forgotten and to achieve the readiness for the transformation that is upon you at this time.

Do not fear that you are not ready or that you are not worthy. We cancel those fears and concerns now and tell you that you are ready, and you are worthy! So now that is out of the way, do not be held back. Charge forward onto the path of growth and transformation with the confidence of a warrior. Do not doubt yourself. You are all capable of participating in this Ascension process and moving forward in your Density levels. Your ultimate goal is to experience the highest level of connection and understanding of the Divine Energy. This is your birthright and will not be denied you.

There are those that would wave their 'magic wand'

and say they have healed your issues for you. Whether they do this with the best of intentions or for monetary gain, they are incorrect. It would be so easy for someone else to say a magic word, or perform some type of ceremony, and complete the work you need to do on yourself for you. Do not fall prey to this belief because it will not happen that way. That is not to say that you cannot go to someone for assistance working on what you need to face and release. As a matter of fact, this is what we mean when we say there are those in physical form to help you. The ones that can truly help you are the ones that know and tell you that they are only supporting your endeavors by offering assistance, but that you are the only one that can actually do the work to free yourself so that you may progress on your Spiritual journey.

We chose this path to reach you because the written word can be powerful; we are infusing our energy with our words to help you understand and support your endeavors to heal yourselves. The spoken word is powerful as well, even more so as the tone we use is filled with the vibrational energy of the Creator. Tone brings the resonance to your physical body in a way reading words are not able to. This is why we are, and will be more frequently, speaking these lessons to those who wish to hear them verbally. Sound therapy is a tangible experience as your physical bodies are simply atoms that are already vibrating at a frequency determined by you. This is what 'raising your vibration' means. You are changing your vibrational frequency as you learn and embody what we are teaching. This then enables you to release the lower vibrational density of the 3rd and move forward to the 4th. You will begin to notice that things that seemed 'normal' no longer 'vibe' with you. You are no longer interested in them or they feel uncomfortable to you because you are beginning to vibrate at a higher frequency that is not compatible with the lower frequency vibration. This is normal and not to be feared. It is why you may find it difficult to be friends with the same people, or you may find it difficult being around family members, and they will not understand the changes in you if they are not also doing the Spiritual work on themselves as you are. We want you to know that these changes are normal and expected. Do not worry at the loss of family or friends. As you raise your vibratory frequency, you will be drawn to others (and they to you) who share the new vibratory frequency that you now inhabit. So, while you might grieve the loss of some of the people in your life, do not dwell there overly long because new adventures await you with your new spiritually aligned family and friends. Rejoice in your progress and turn to help others on their journey, as there were those that have helped you.

# À Tout À L'heure

That is all for now. We have given you much to think about and much to remember and to master. Remember, you are the shaper of your own destiny! What we give you is possible to accomplish. To summarize the homework that we are giving to you:

1. Begin your Meditation practice

As we have stated, it is not the act of meditating that is important but the FEELING you obtain from doing it. Find that 'thing' that you love doing (walking/sitting in the woods, crafting, coloring etc.) that allows your Mind to let go its control. Allow thoughts to come and go and be in the peaceful calm that drops you from occupying your Mind to your Heart Center where we can communicate with you. When you are in your Heart Center rather than your Mind, you are existing in the Now. Learn to recognize this FEELING and practice it daily. Close your eyes for a moment, envision you are in that moment again, and slip into your Heart Center. Do this as often as you wish (but at least once a day), and every time that you feel you have gone back into your Mind. This does not need to be an overly long process. When you have more time to spend, you may wish to do so. Otherwise, the goal of this exercise is to conjure the FEELING that drops you into your Heart Center and would only take a few minutes of your time. This is a wonderful way to begin your day in a calm, centered place.

2. Cleanse your Energy and Hold your Space

At least once daily, use the grounding technique we spoke of and wash the energy of others, and your old stagnant energy, out of your body with a shower of pure radiant light. Ask us to help you hold your space, the bubble of radiant light that surrounds your physical body, and to heal any damage to your aura. This is important to do daily, especially as you raise your vibration because as your vibration rises your light shines even brighter and you become a beacon for those entities that are attracted, like moths to a flame, but are not there for your best or highest good. Also, holding your space with a brilliant light and keeping your aura healthy and strong ensures that only entities of the Light (that are there for your Highest Good) are able to have access to you. As a part of this step, remember to ask your guides and Angels to help with anything they can, so that we are able to step in and help without overriding your Free Will. This is also important to do daily. If you have time for only one, this or meditation, then do this. This is a good way to begin a meditation, but can be done anytime and multiple times a day. Any time you are feeling overly stressed, close your eyes and go through this routine and you will immediately start to feel calmer as the beautiful and brilliant light washes through you and you feel the comfort of the Creator surround you.

3. Practice Non-Judgment

This is a good place to start in achieving all three: Unconditional Love, Unconditional Forgiveness, and Unconditional Non-Judgment. It is really the cornerstone of the foundation. Remember, even the smallest of Judgments will hold you back from accomplishing all three, which is the requirement of the Creator for your graduation to the next 'grade in school'. Recognize when you are having a judgmental thought, and then let it go and forgive yourself. Do not participate when others are making judgmental comments about someone else. When you begin to recognize how often you are making judgmental comments or having judgmental thoughts, you will be astounded to see how often others are too. Do not fall into judging others for their judgmental comments. Observe and forgive, and in that way you are offering Unconditional Love.

4. Practice Detachment from Outcomes

This is an important step to practice. If you are not able to let go of judging outcomes as *good* or *bad, right* or *wrong,* and allow them to be neutral, then you will never be able to let go of judging yourself or anyone else. And it is a requirement for you to release all forms of judgment. Not only that, you free yourselves from tyranny by healing yourself of the need to judge. When you experience the Detachment from Outcomes, you experience a freedom like you have never known before. You can just BE, simply

BE, without the burden of the chains of Judgment. As the child in our previous example, you are able to move from one experience to another simply appreciating the value of the experience before moving on to another. This was the original intention of experiencing the Earth and it is vital that you break old habits and return to the neutrality of outcomes.

These are the vital points we give you to practice until we meet again. We hope that you have found this information helpful and the tools that we give you useful. Do not expect yourself to learn these things overnight. It takes time to change habits. Give yourself time to learn and to practice this material, and practice forgiveness for yourself in the times that you do not get it quite right. The more you practice these new ways of living, the easier and more natural it will become. The growth you see in yourself will amaze you! Just stick with it and remember to always ask us for help and we are there with you.

Printed in the United States
By Bookmasters